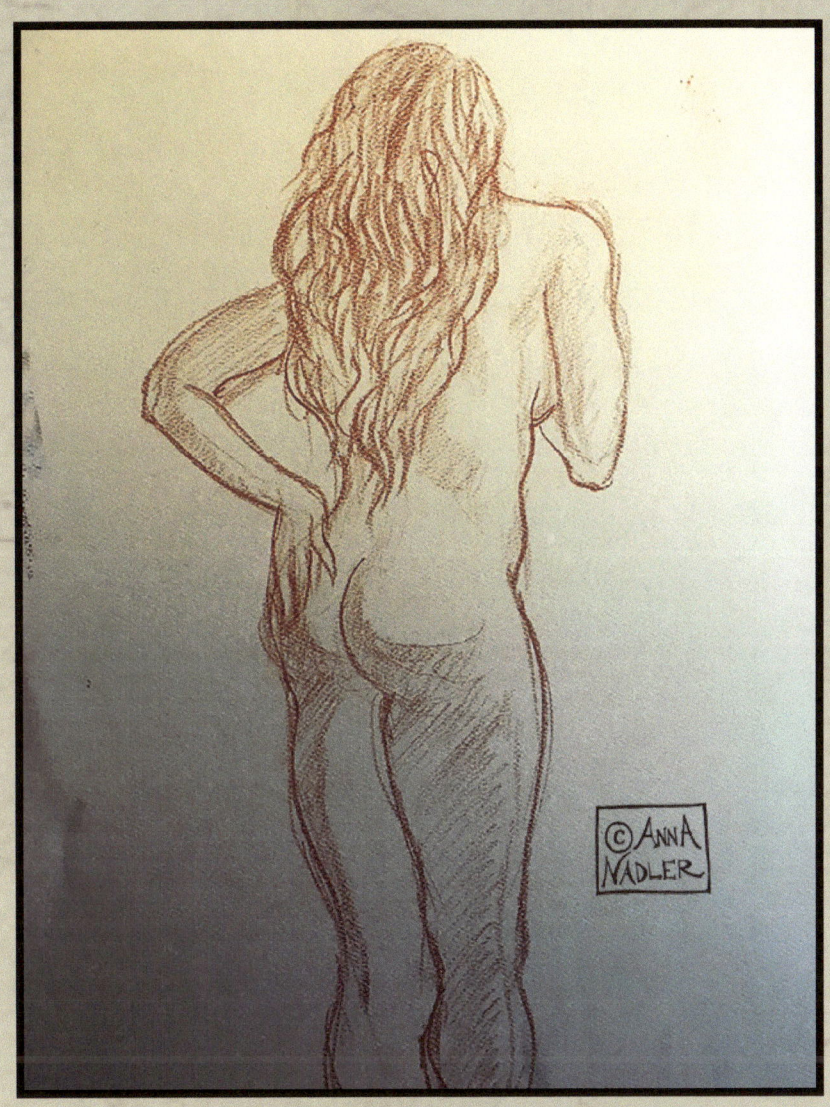

Welcome to "Drawing the Female Form."
Here you will see a collection of life drawings done on location at different art studios in New York City, over a span of about five years. The mediums used in the drawings include pencil, pen, watercolor, marker and pastel. i hope you enjoy this book!
Thank you!

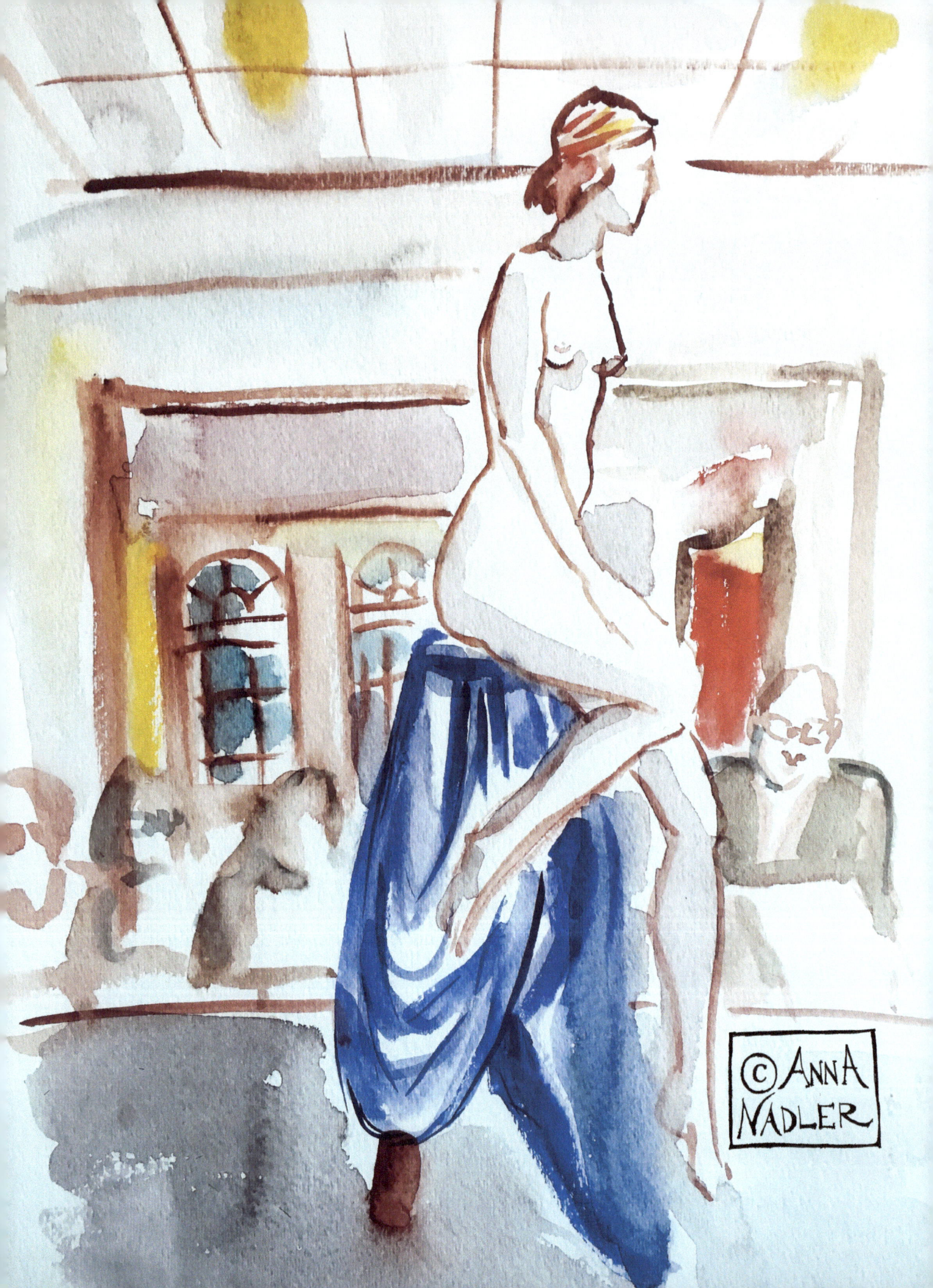

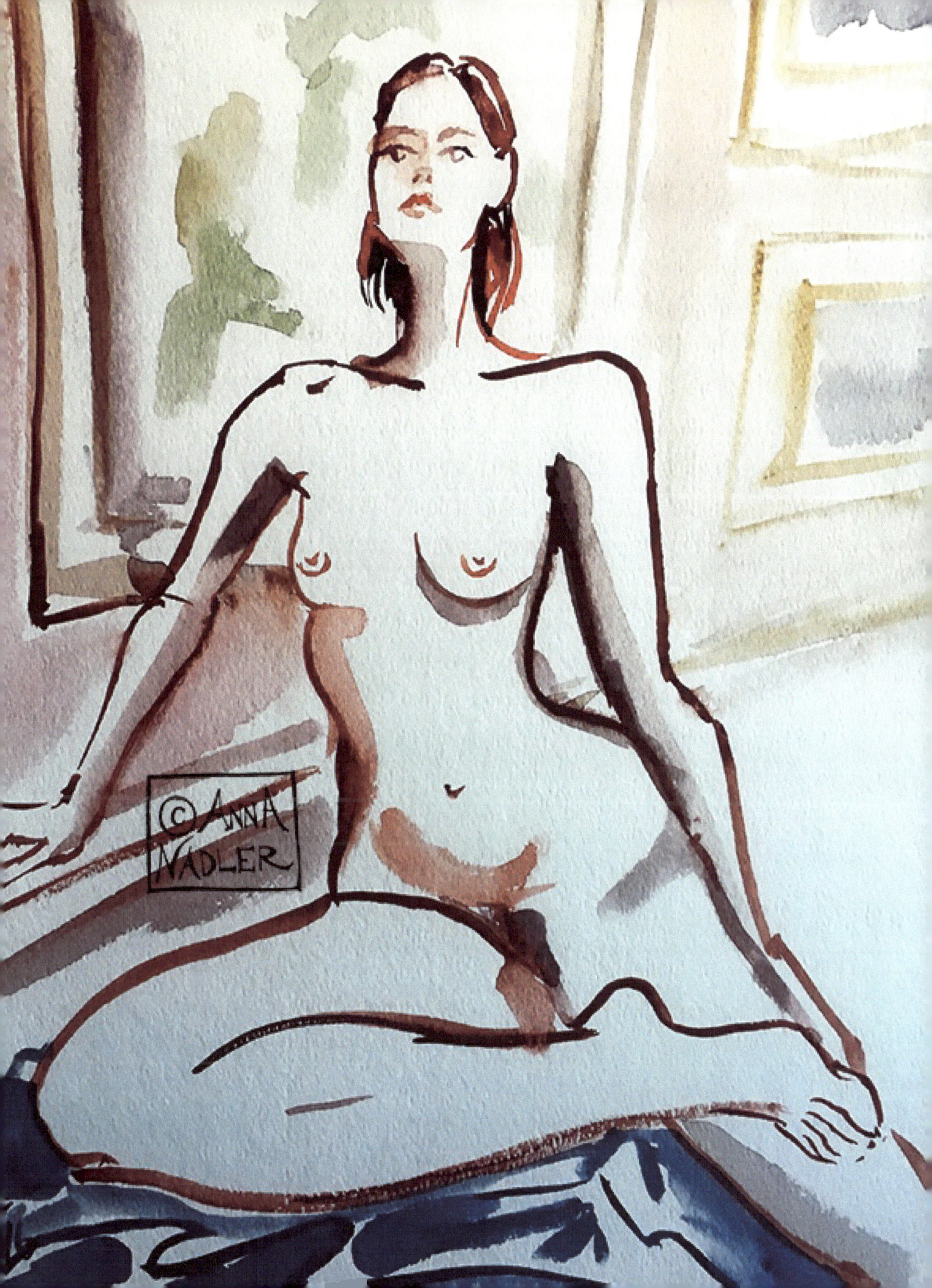

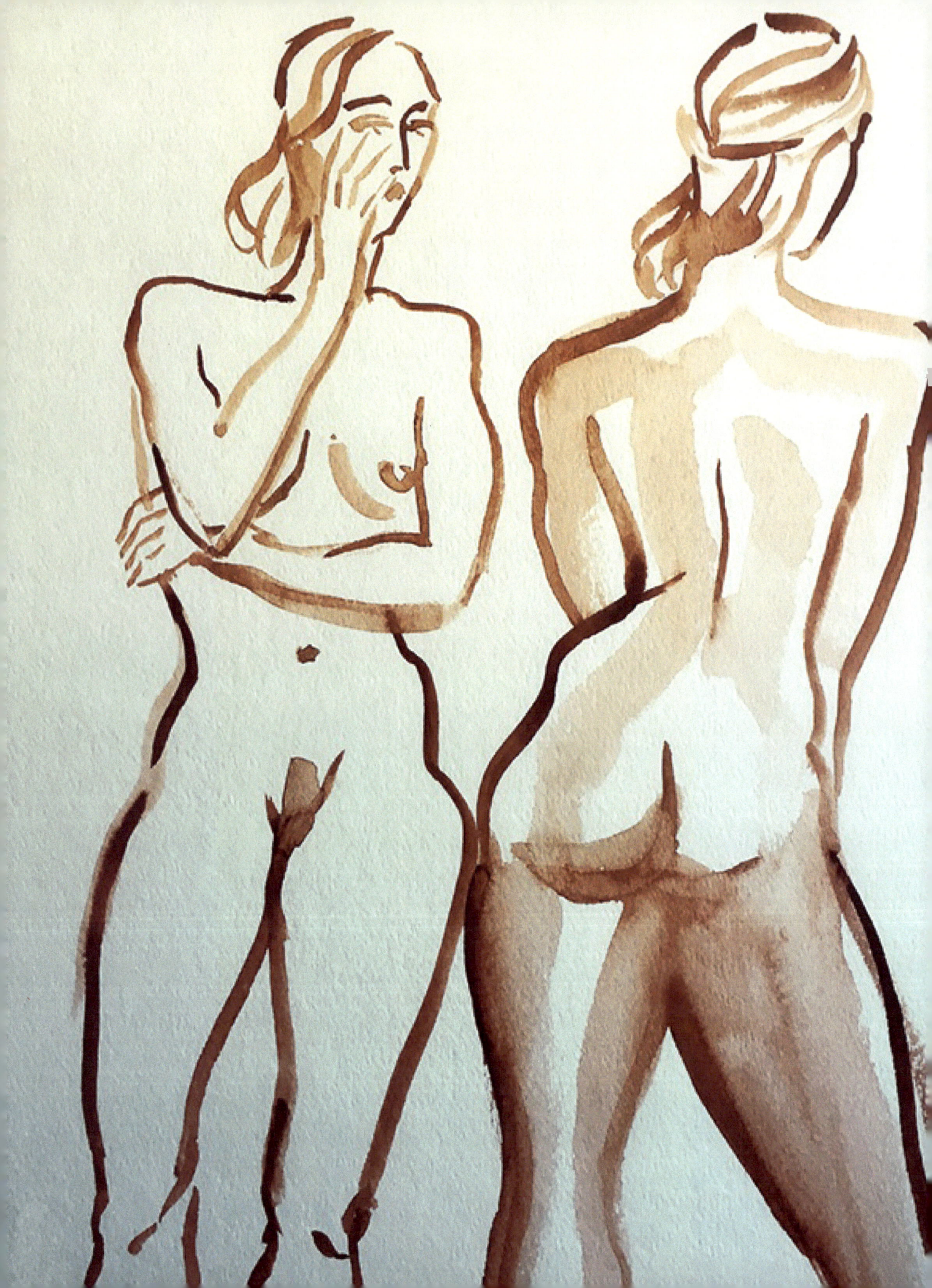

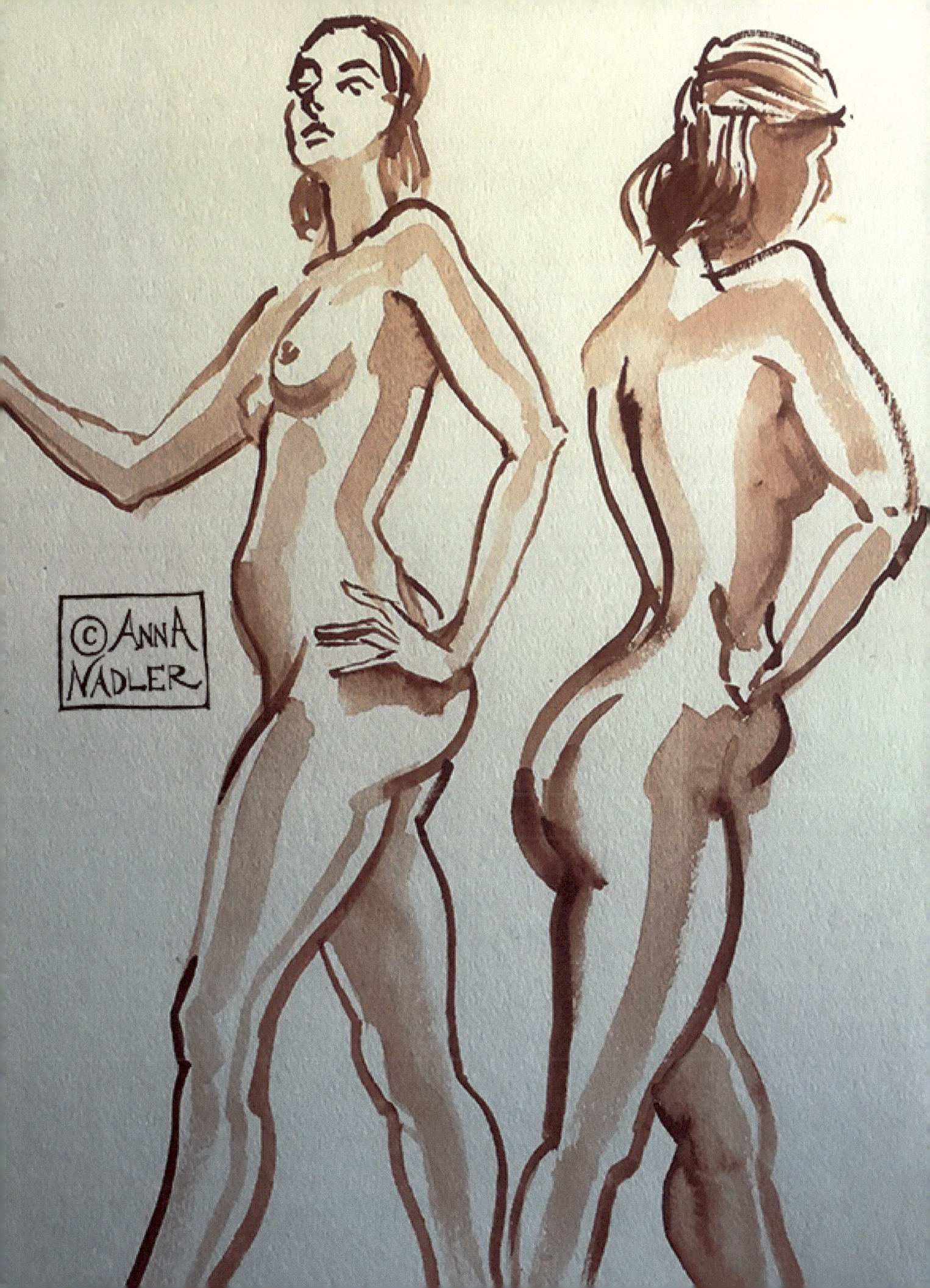

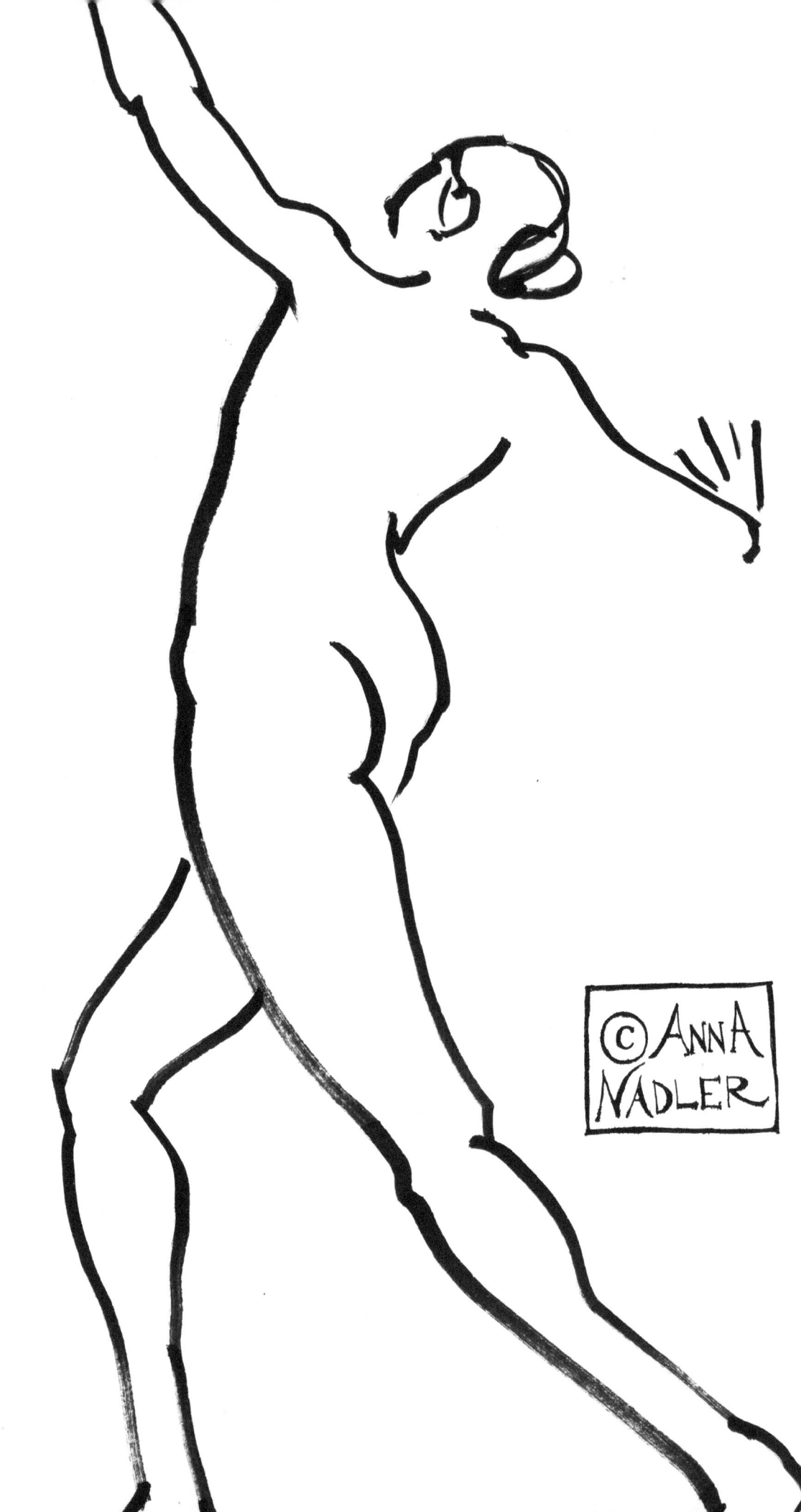

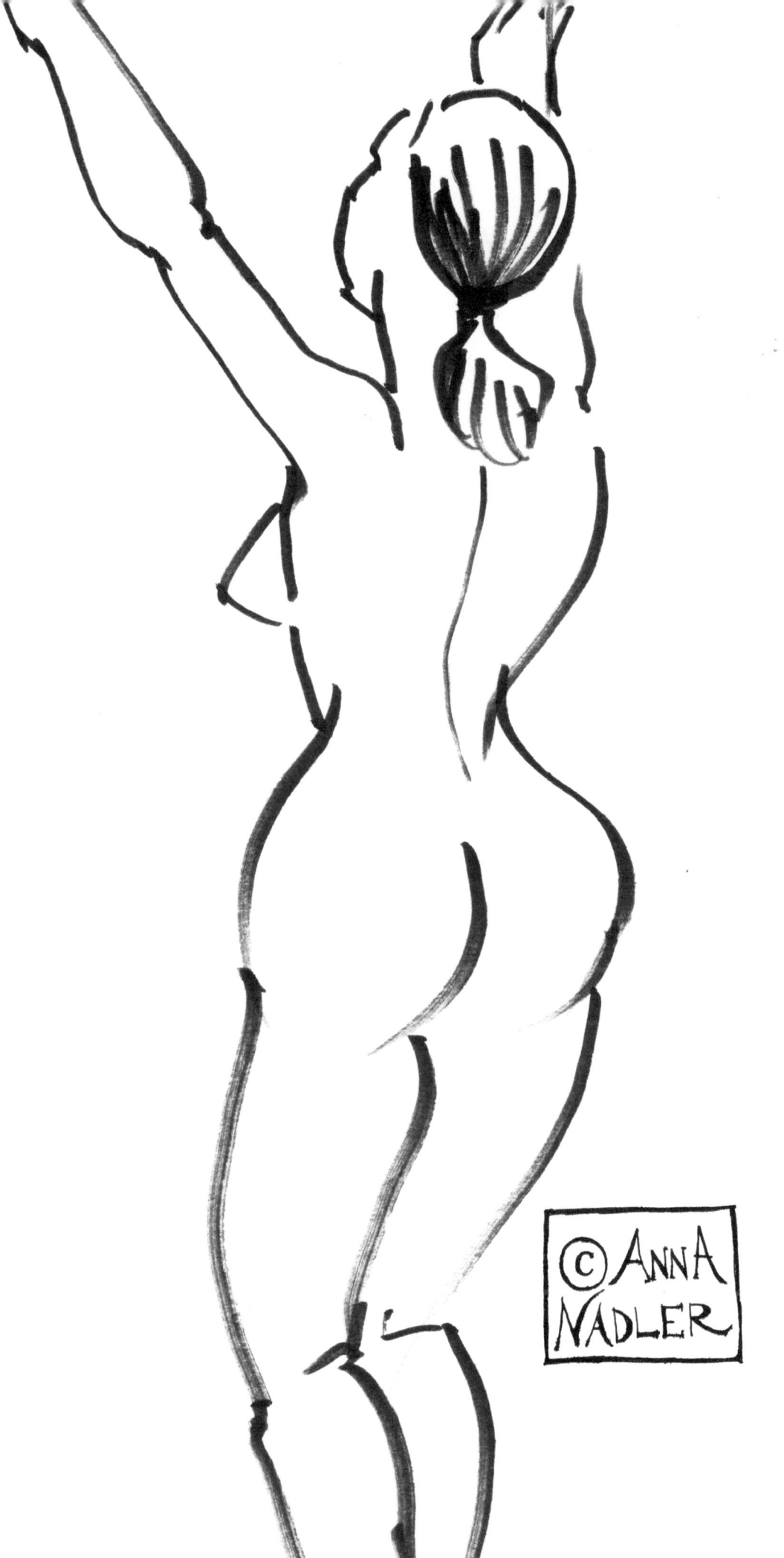

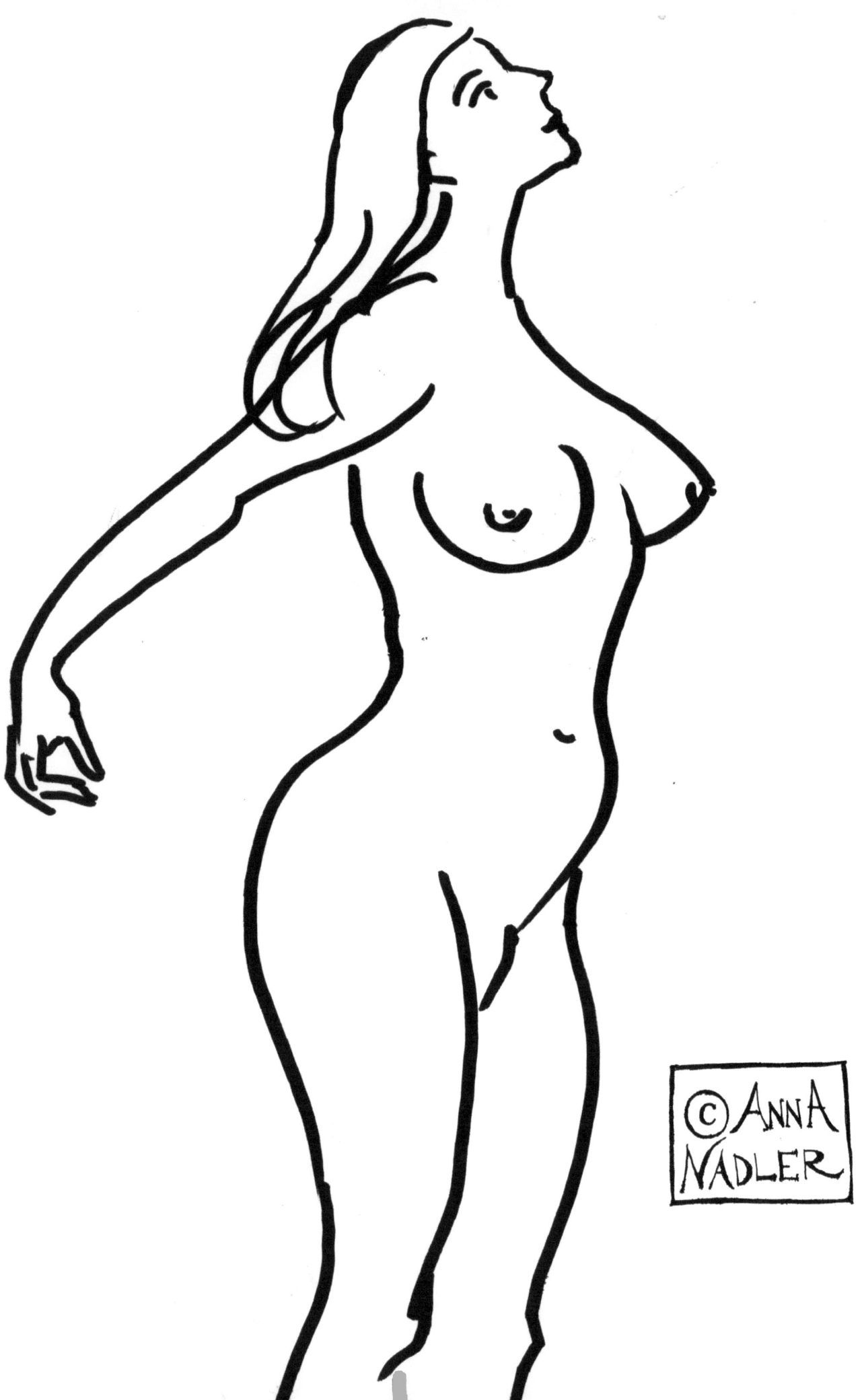

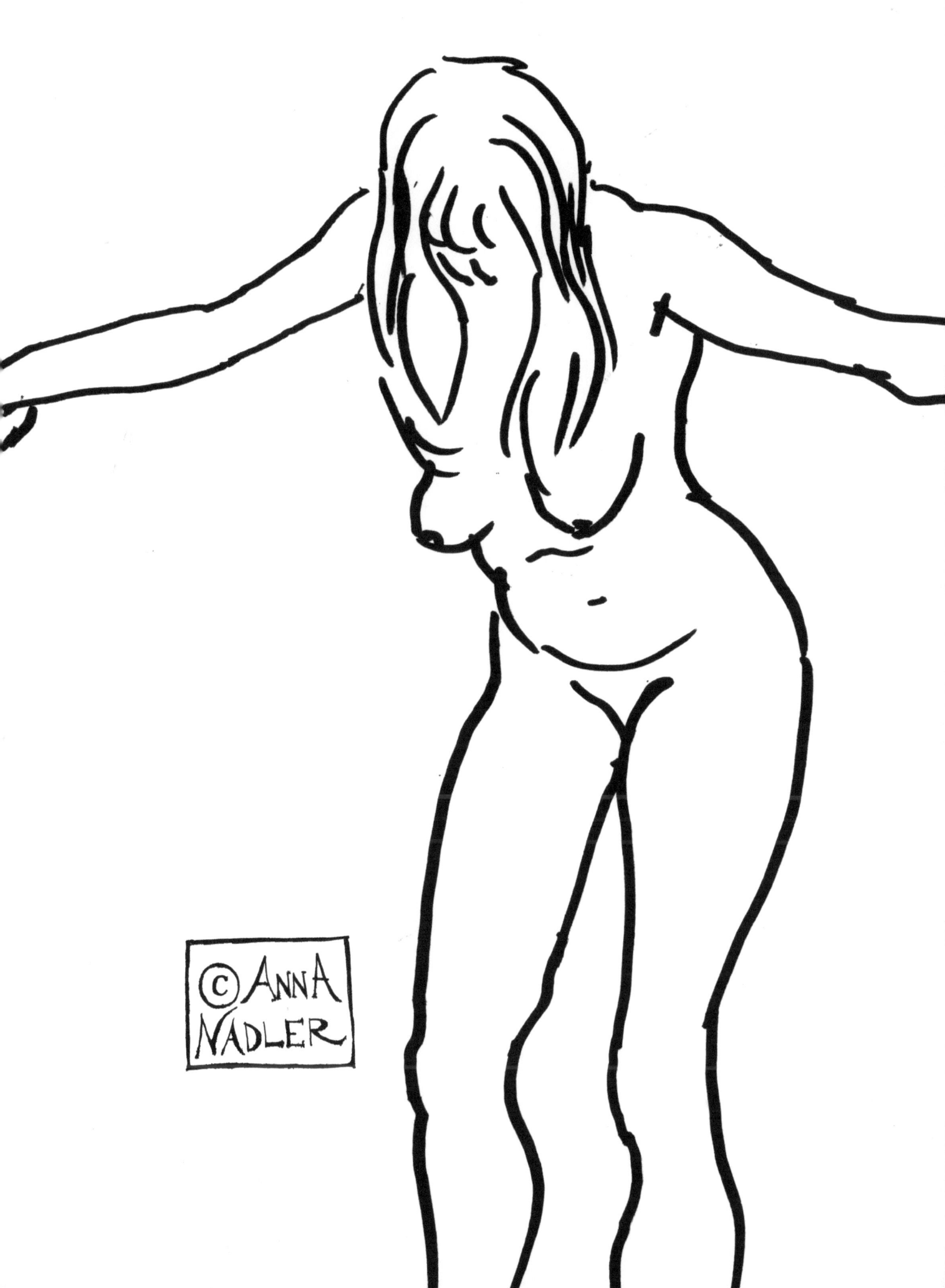

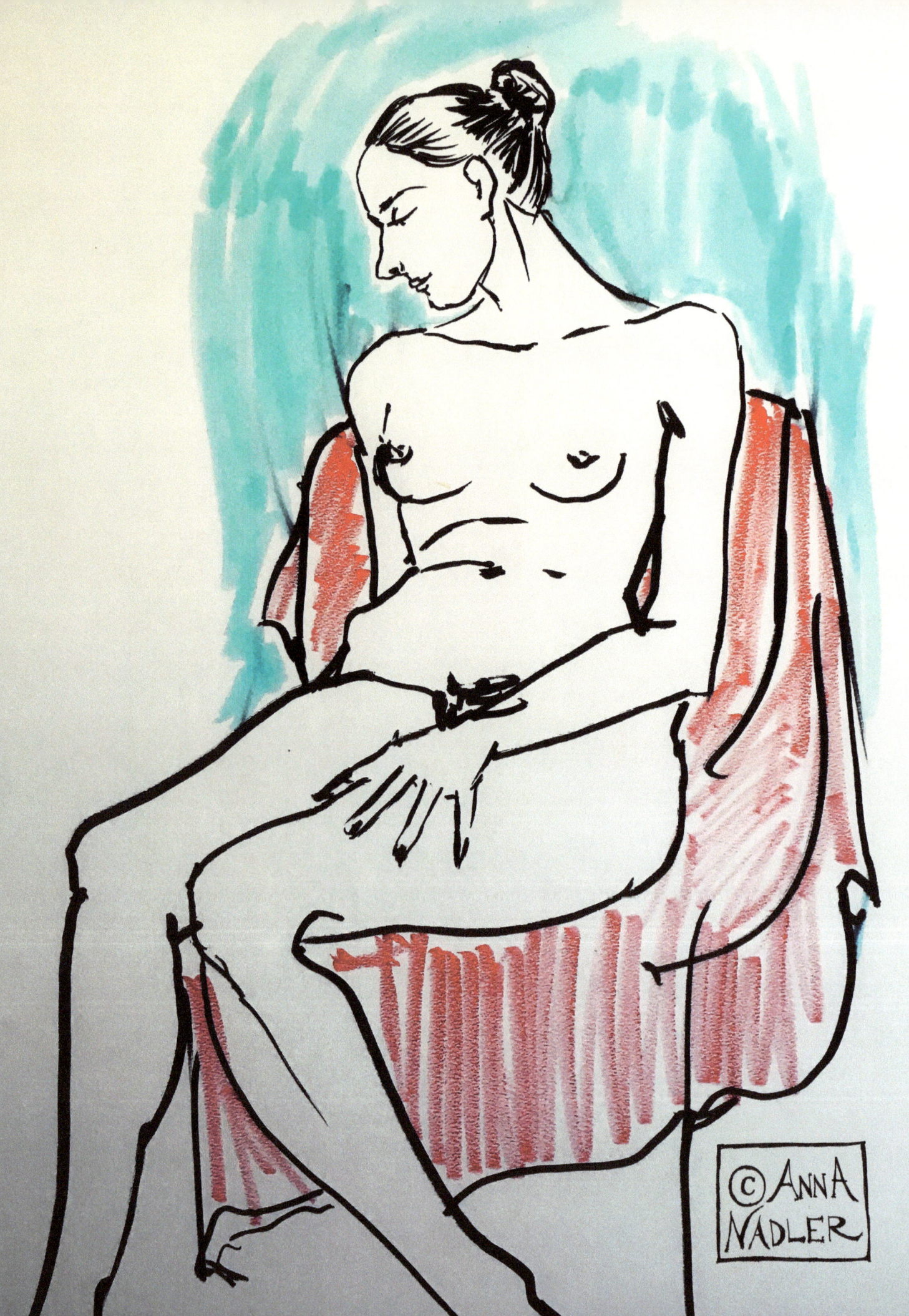

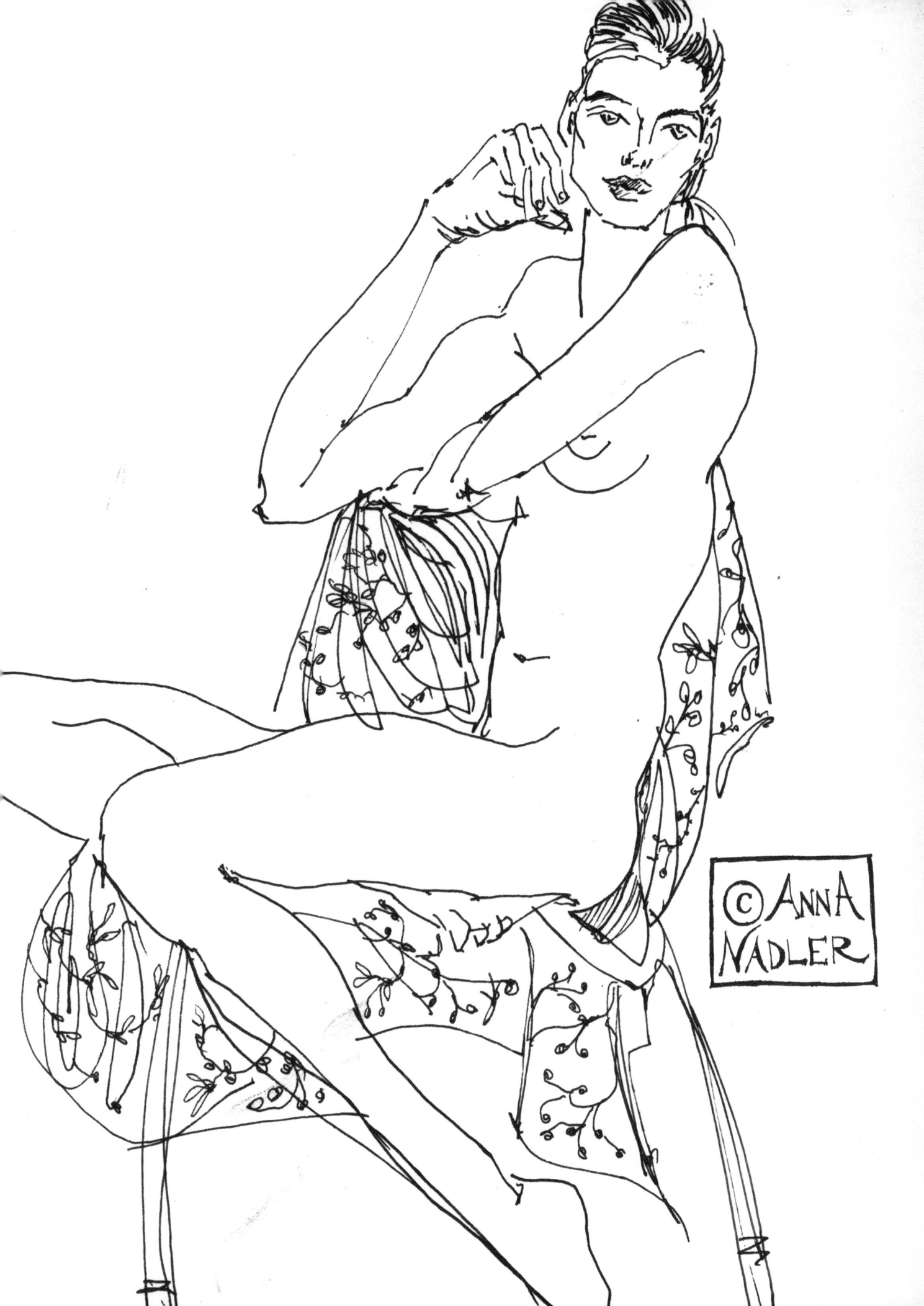

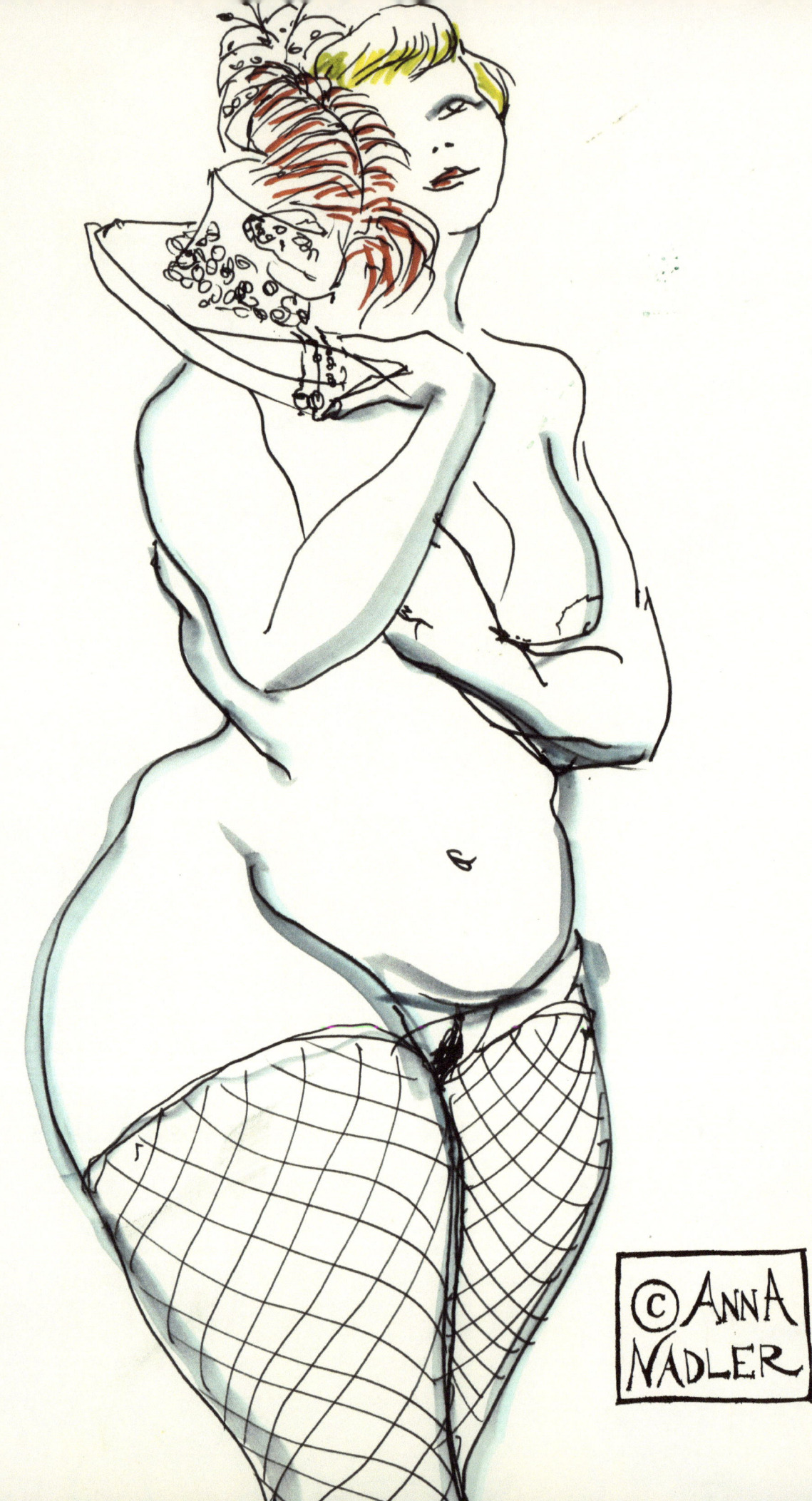

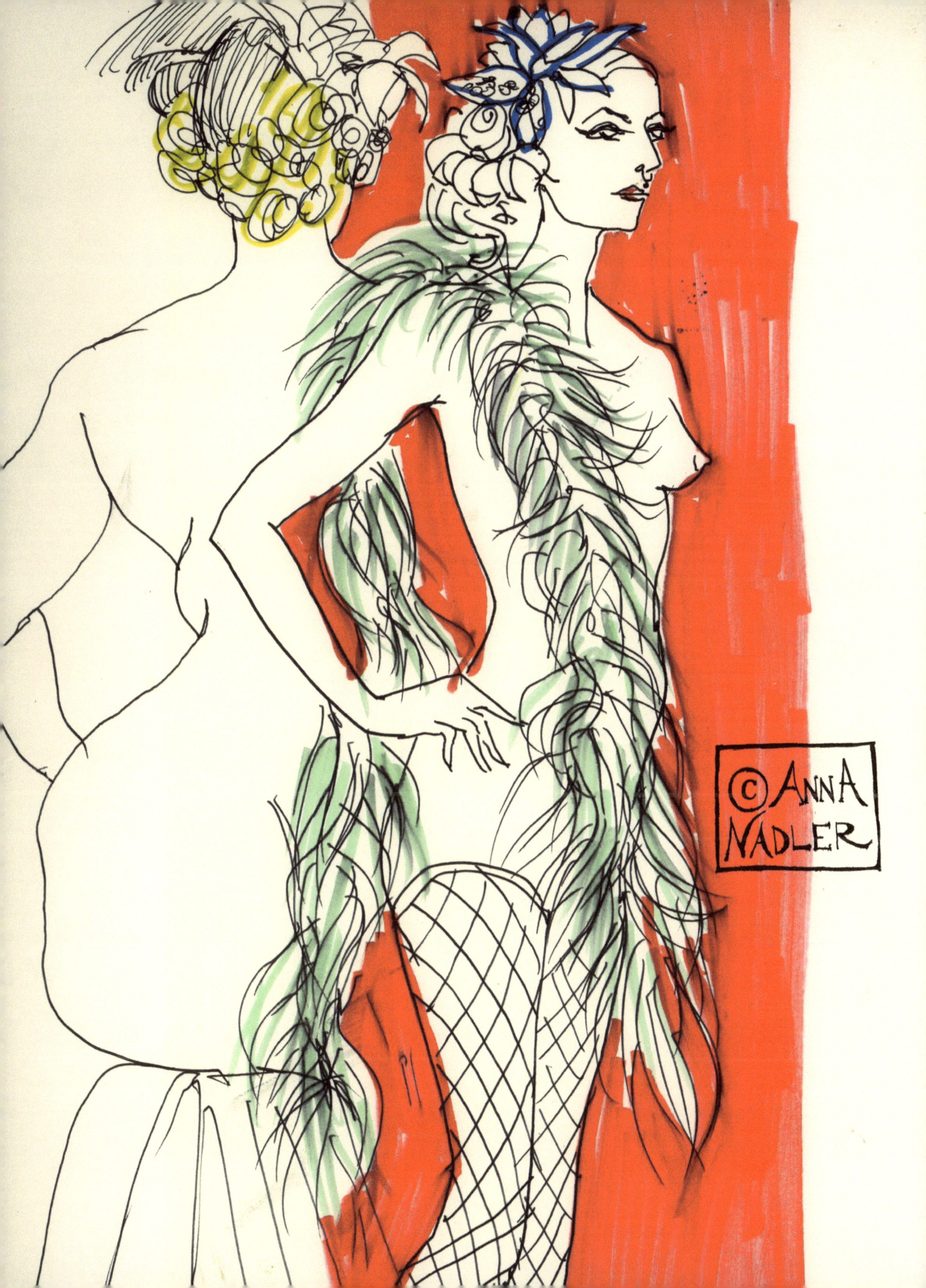

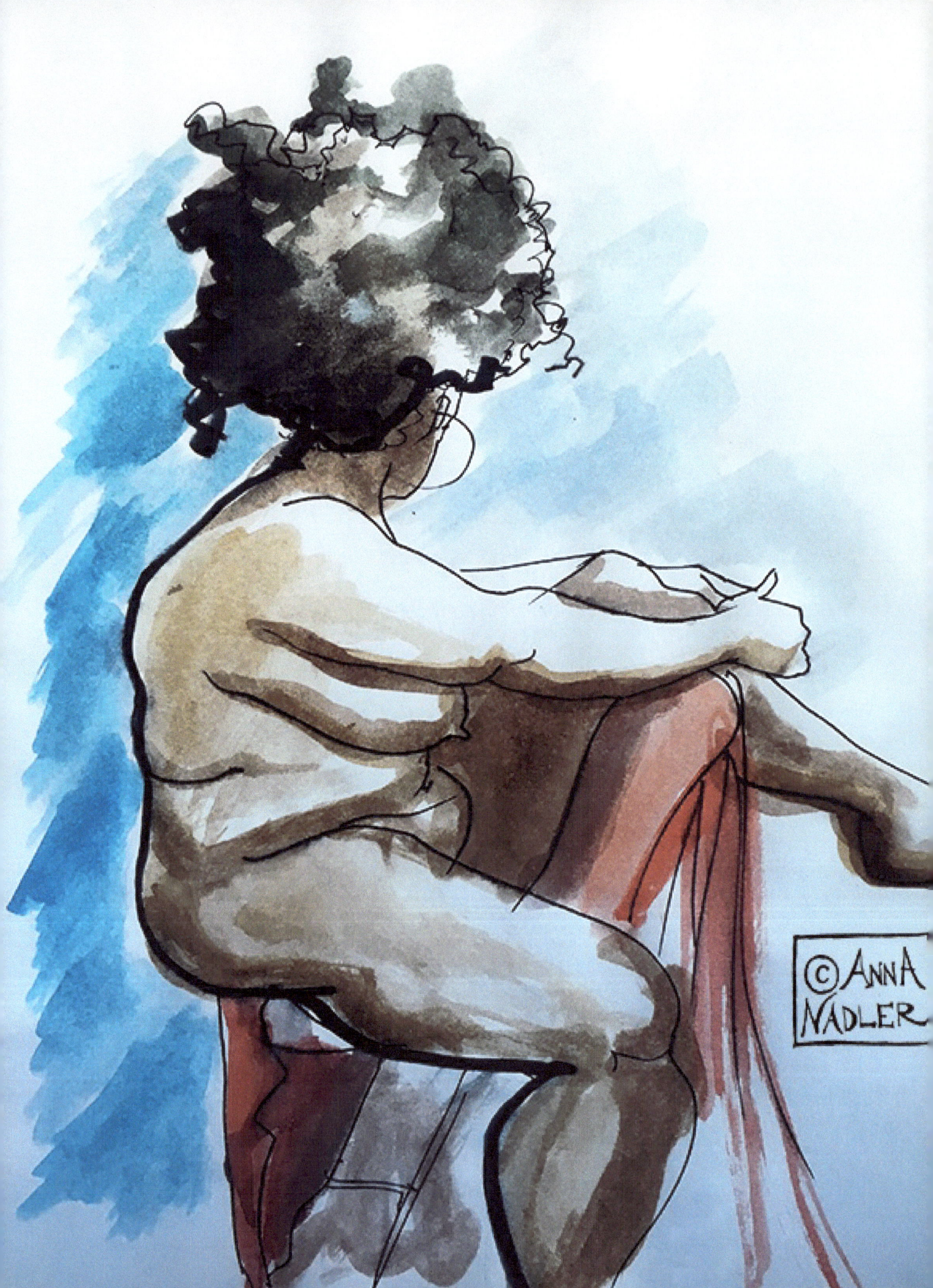

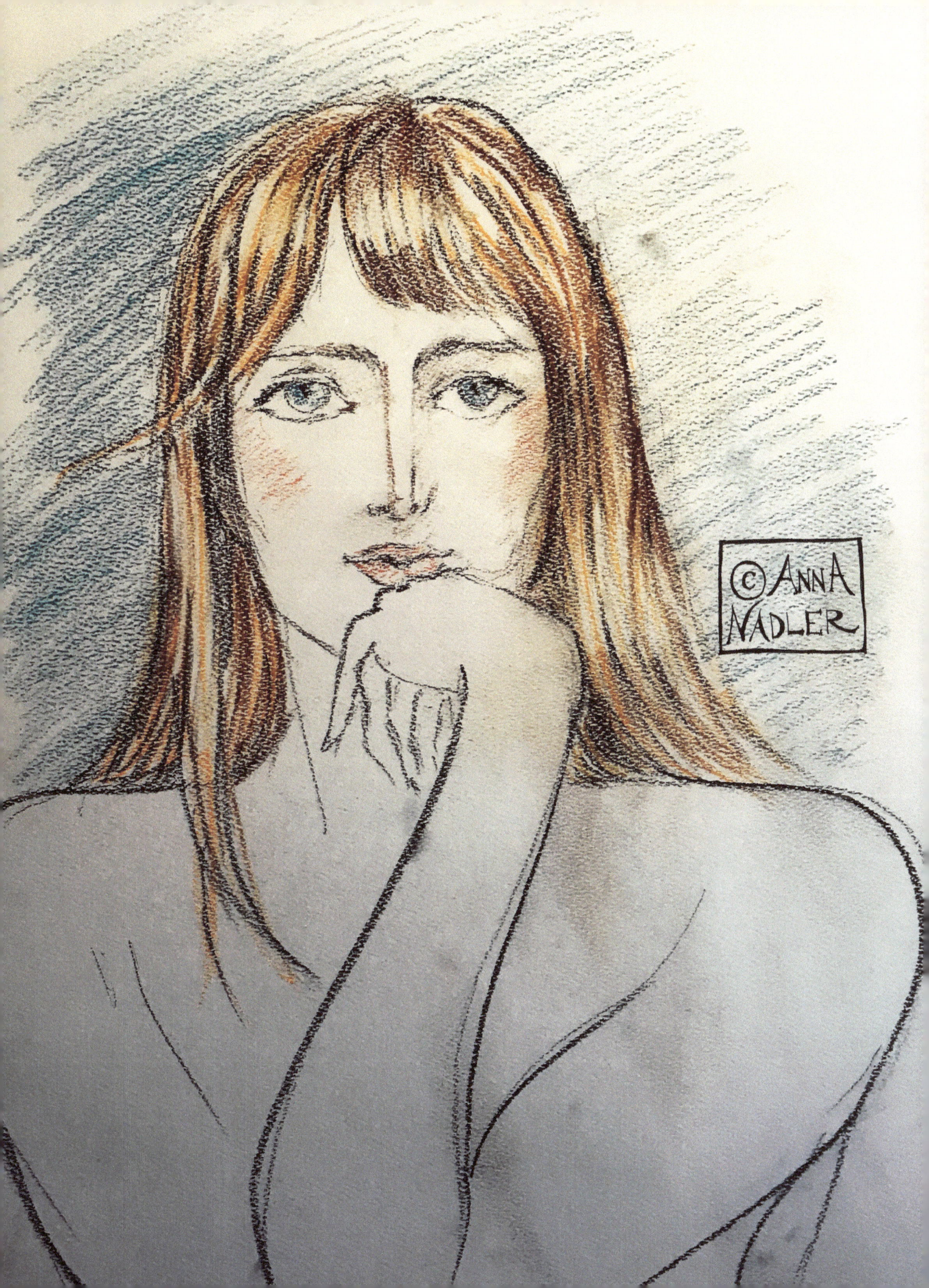

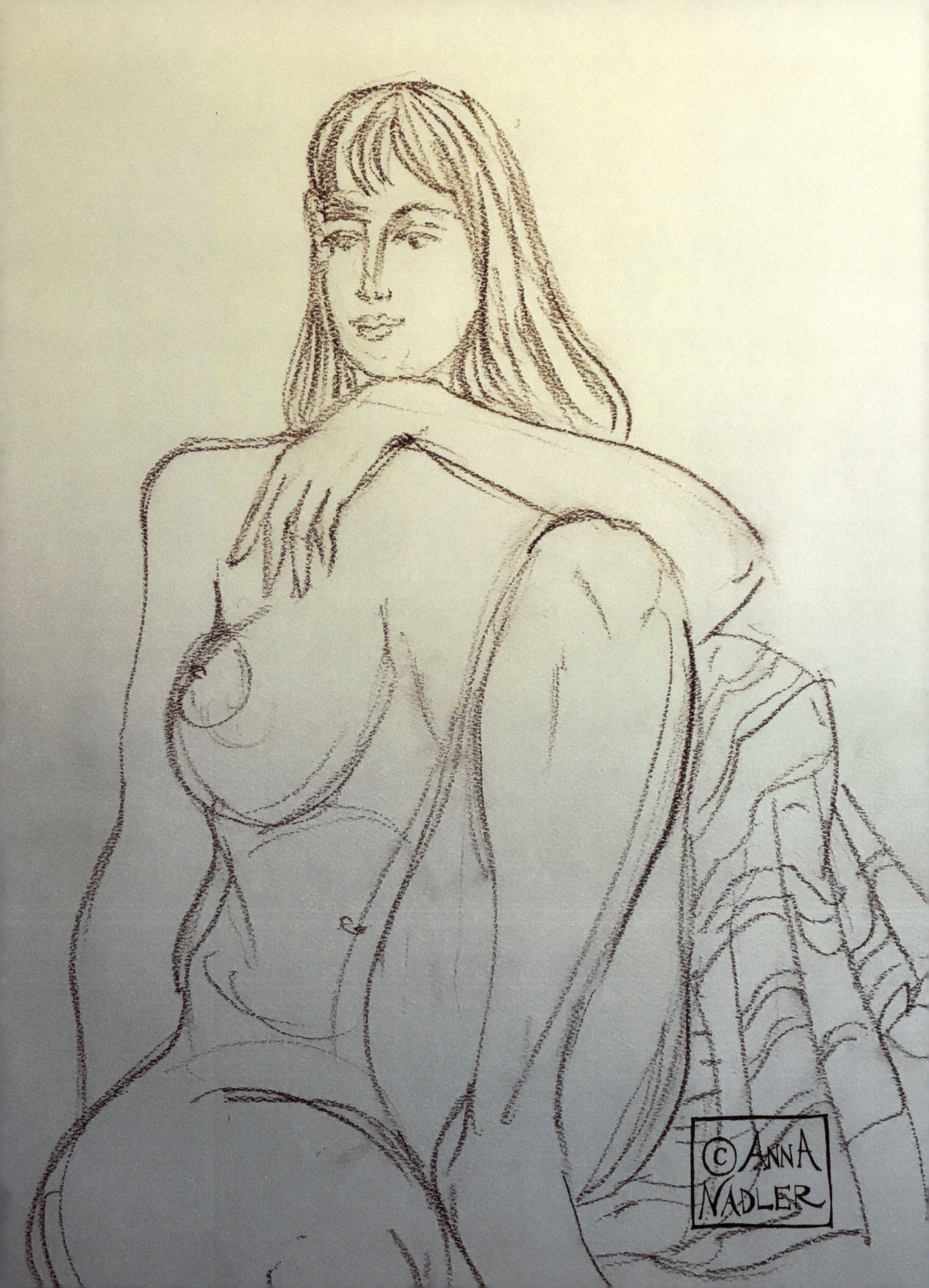

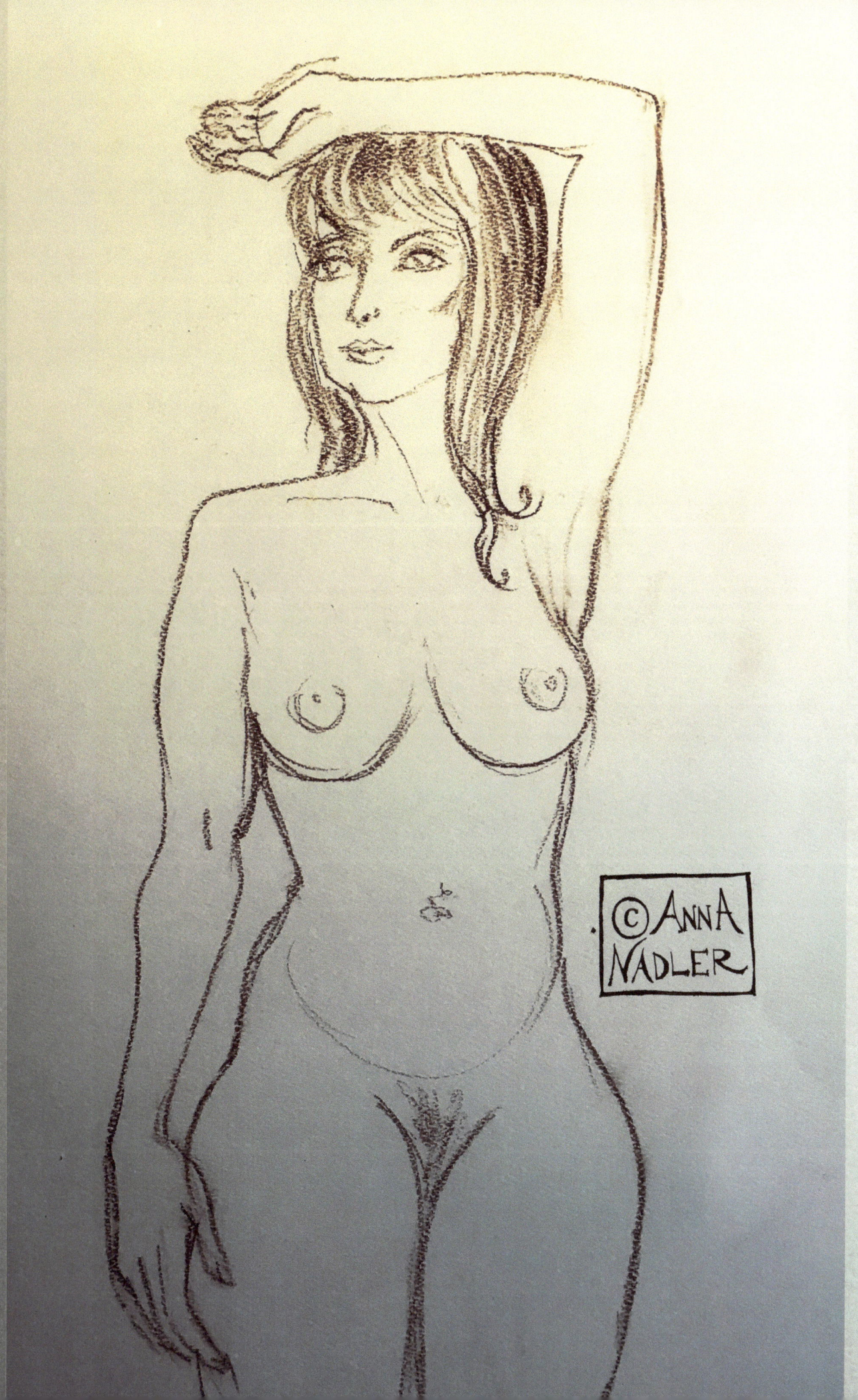

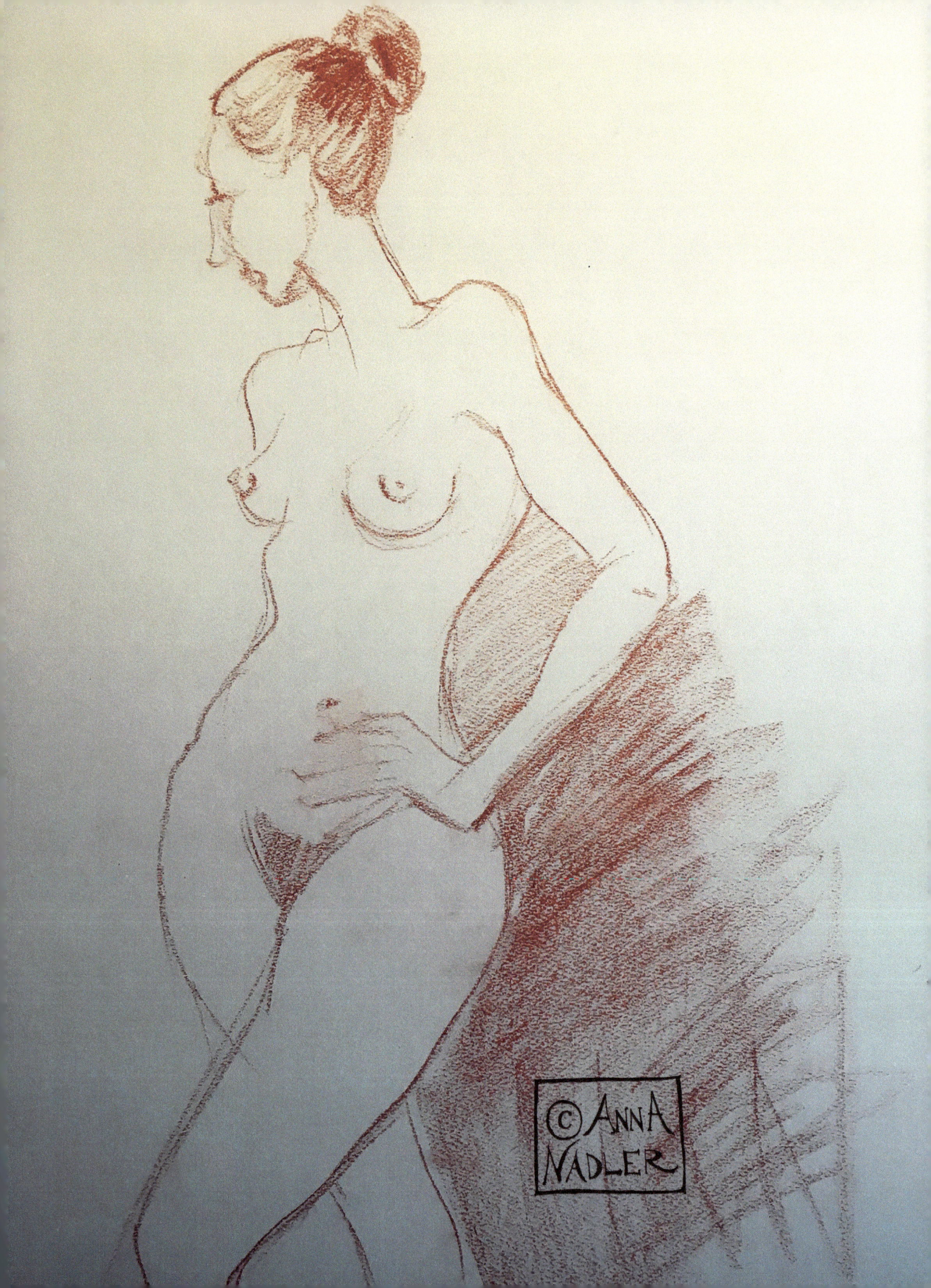

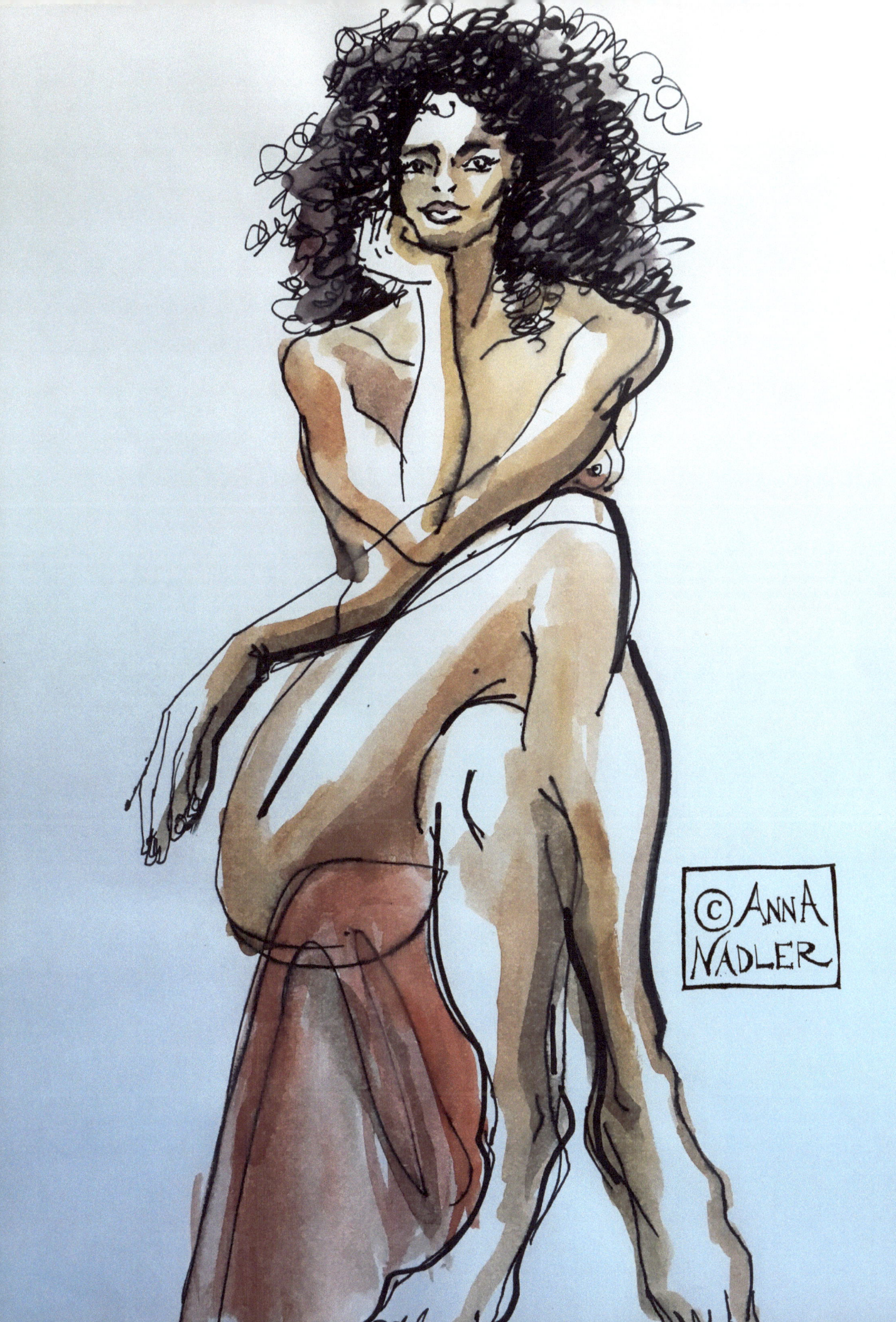

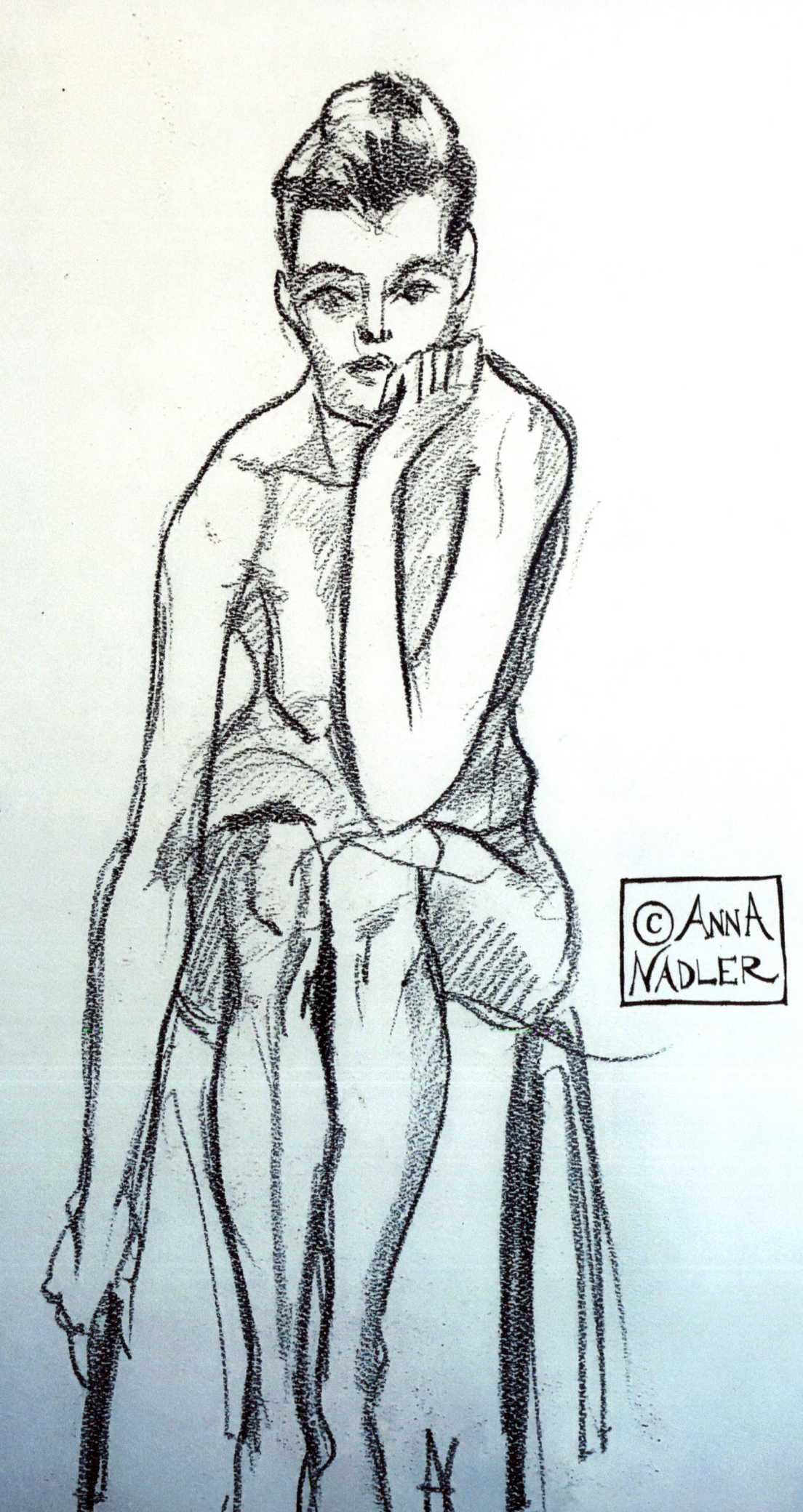

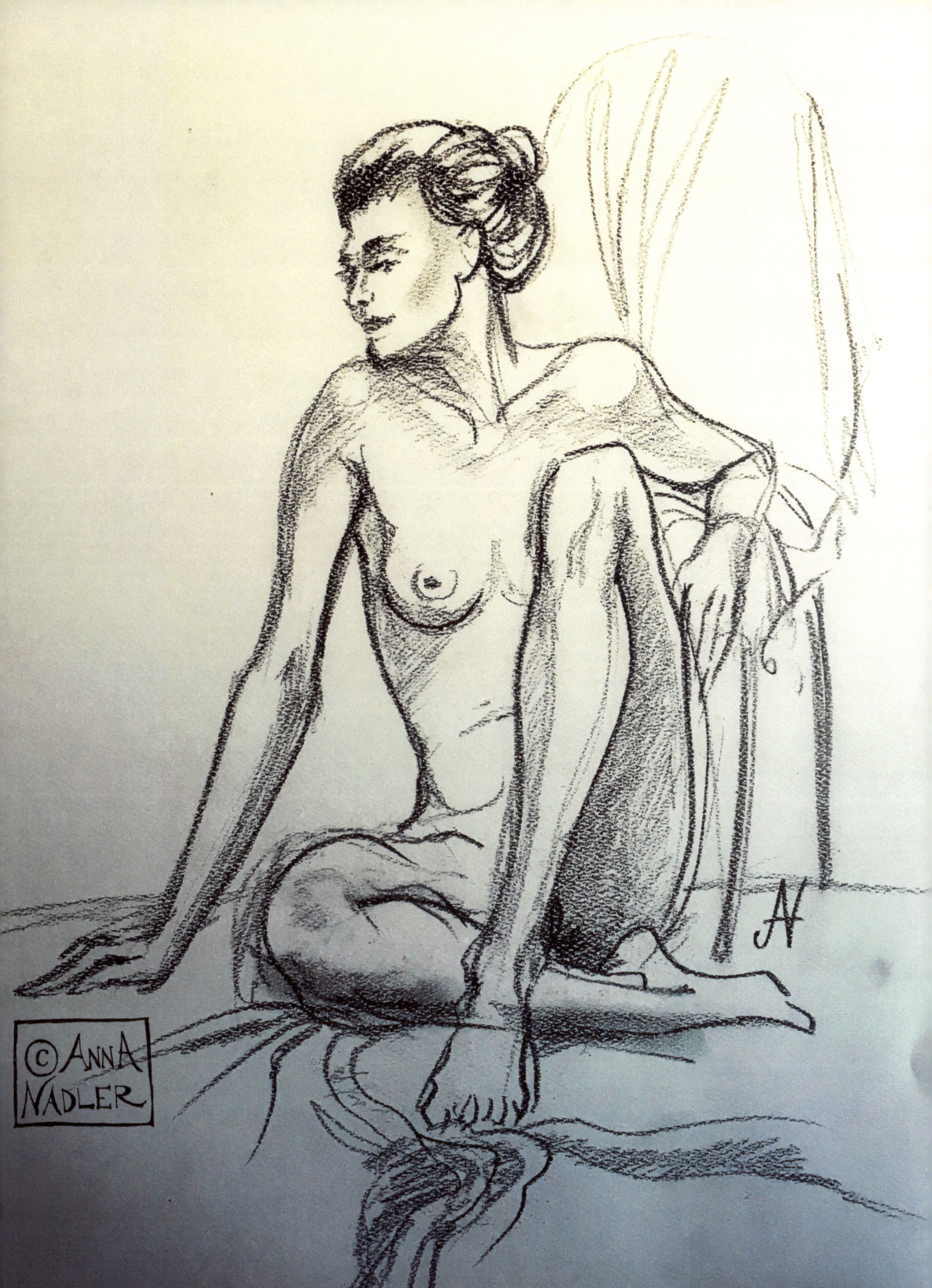

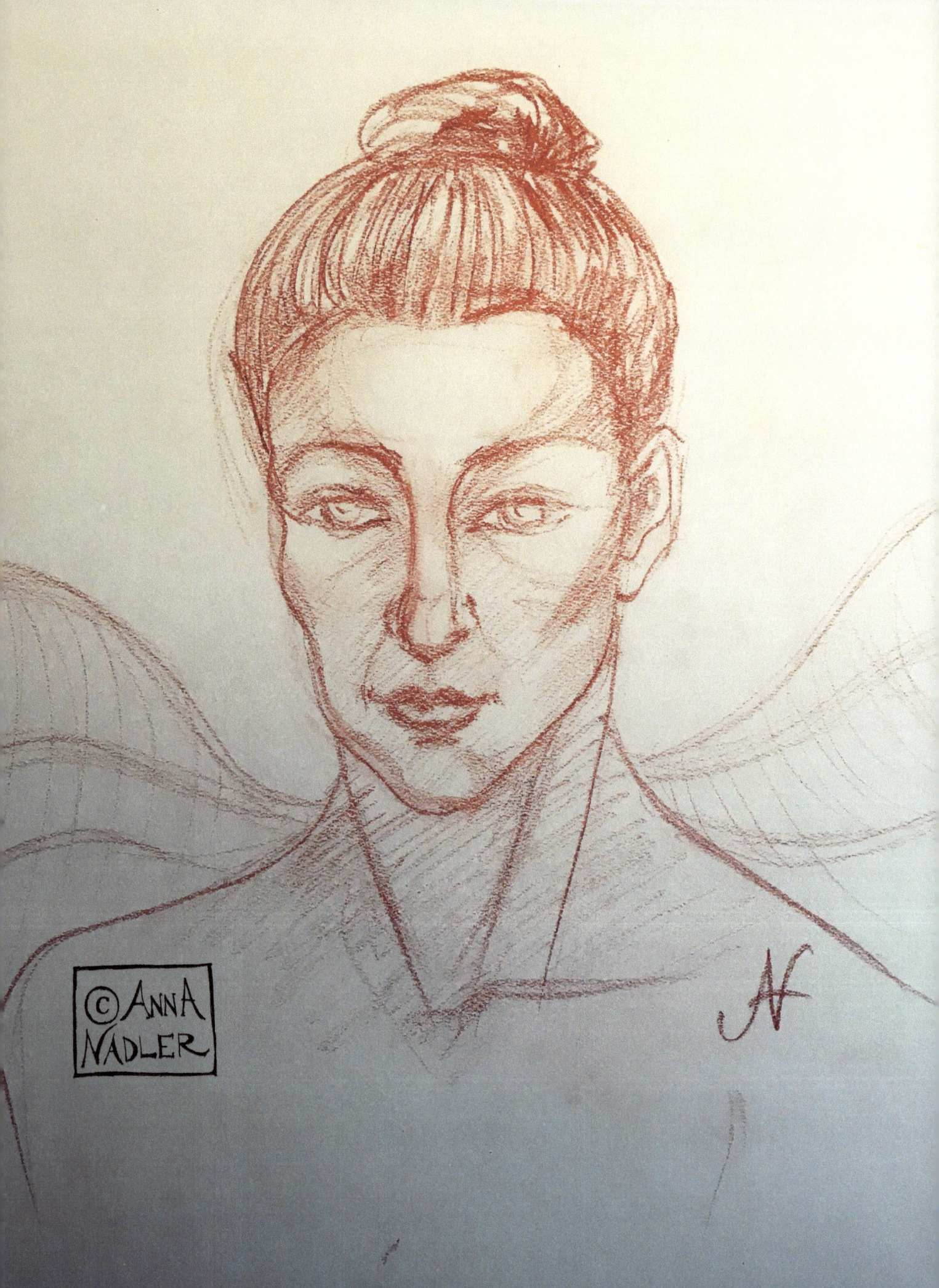

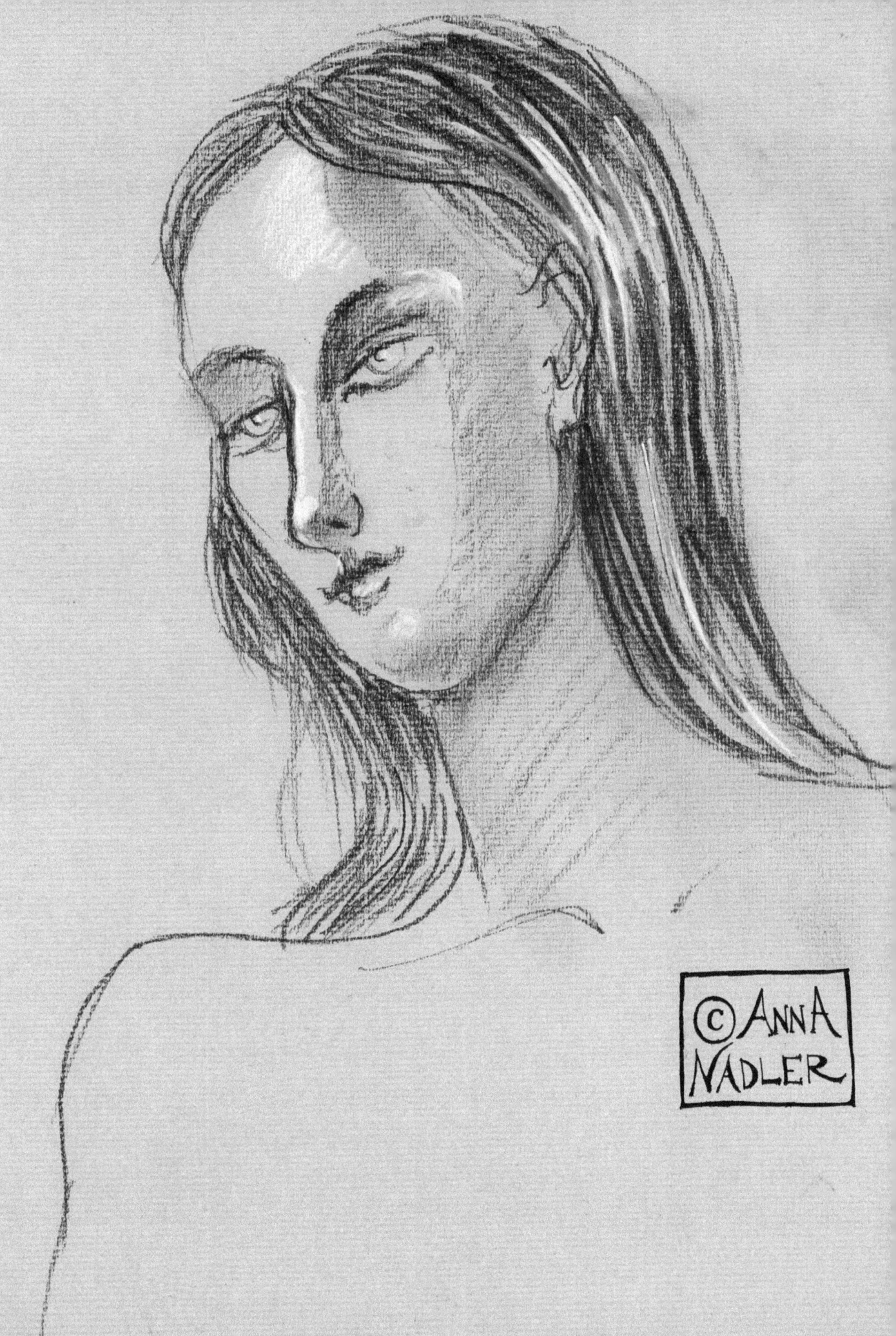

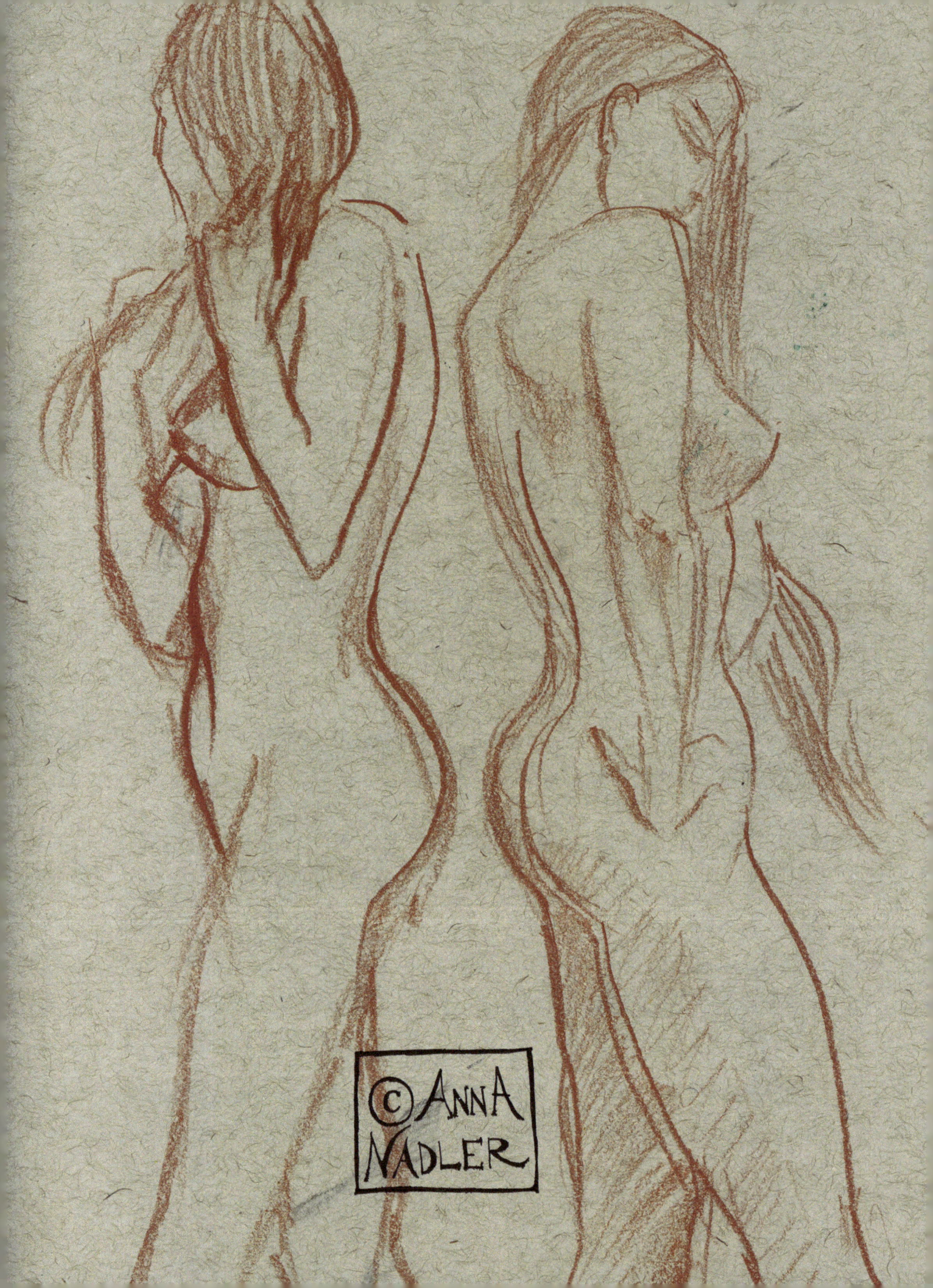

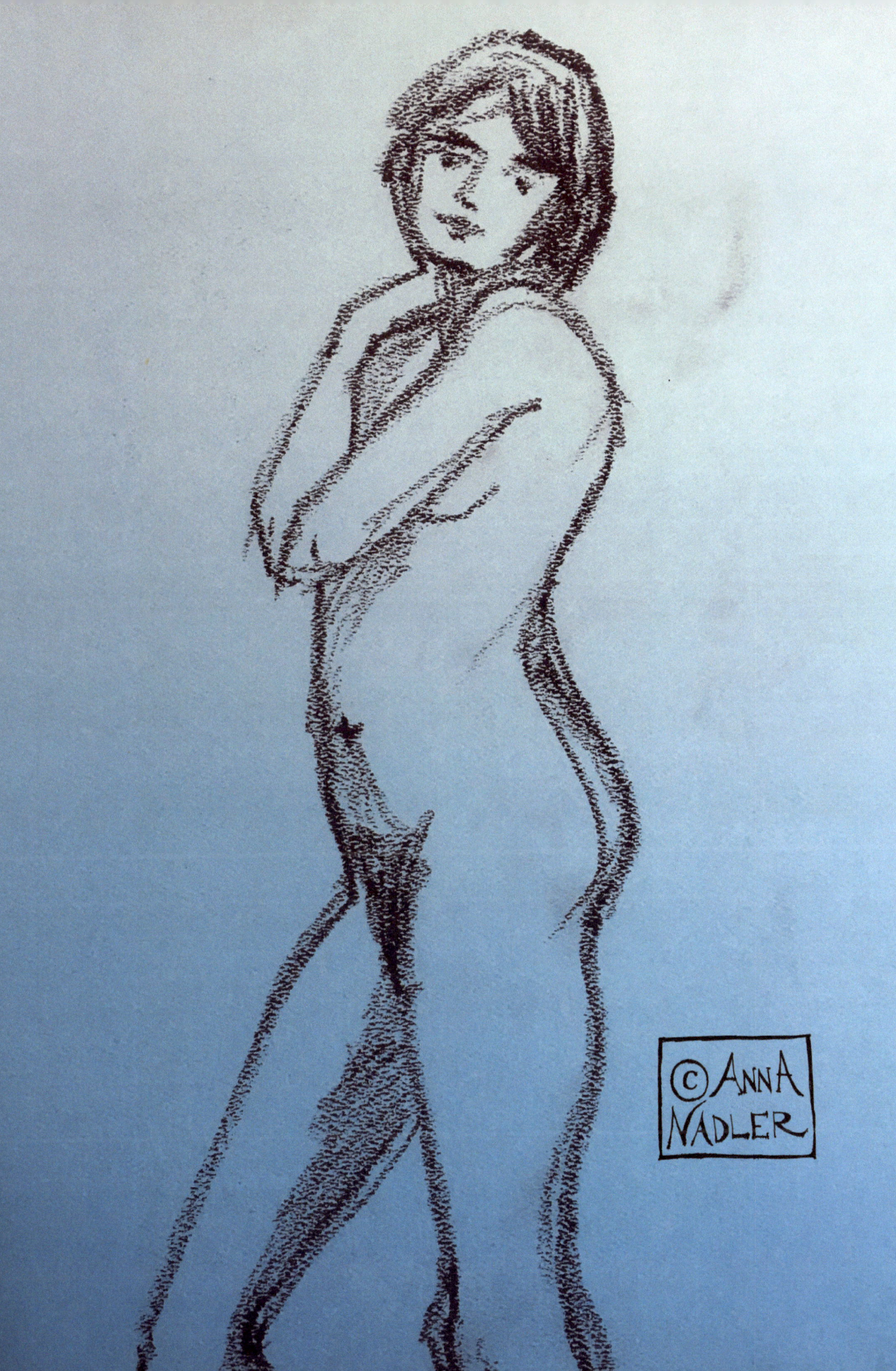

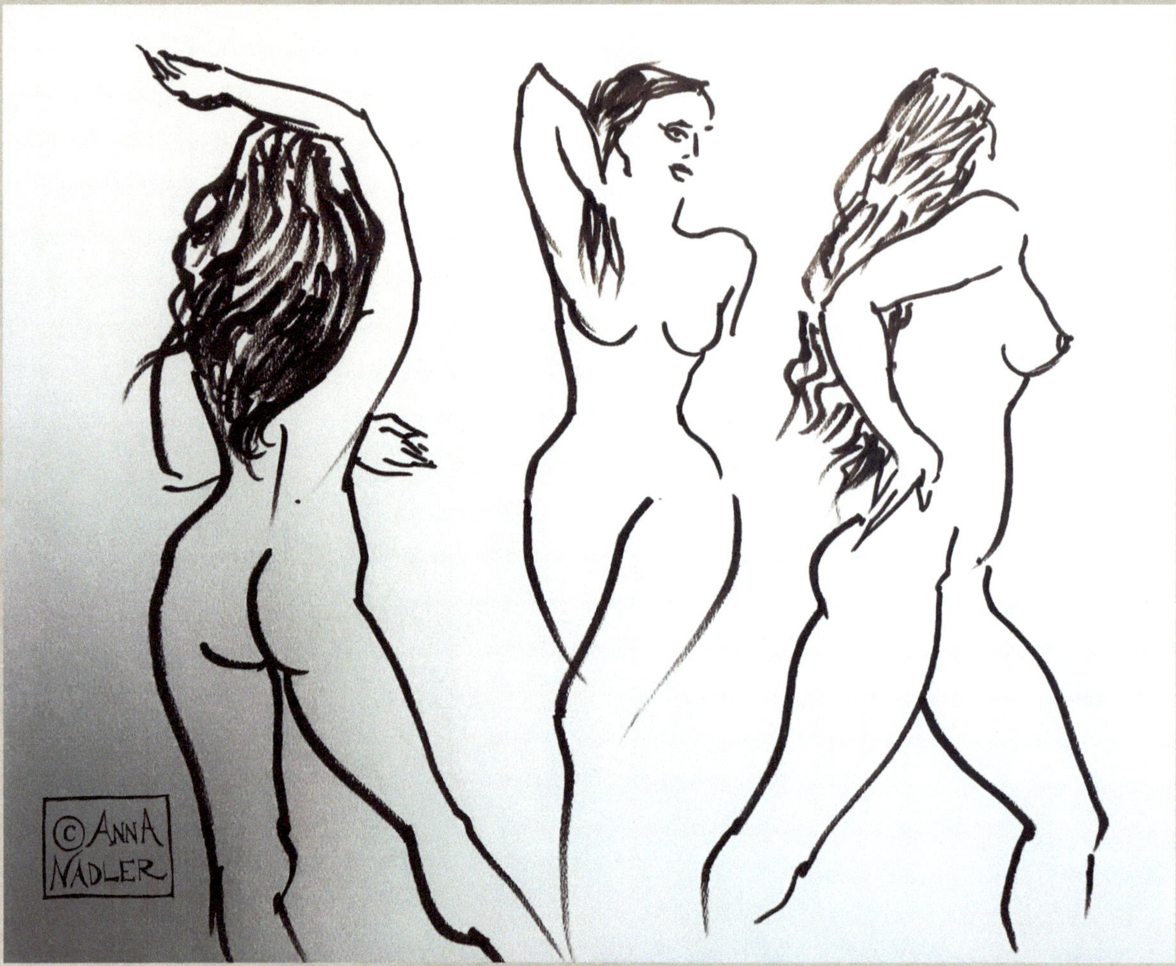

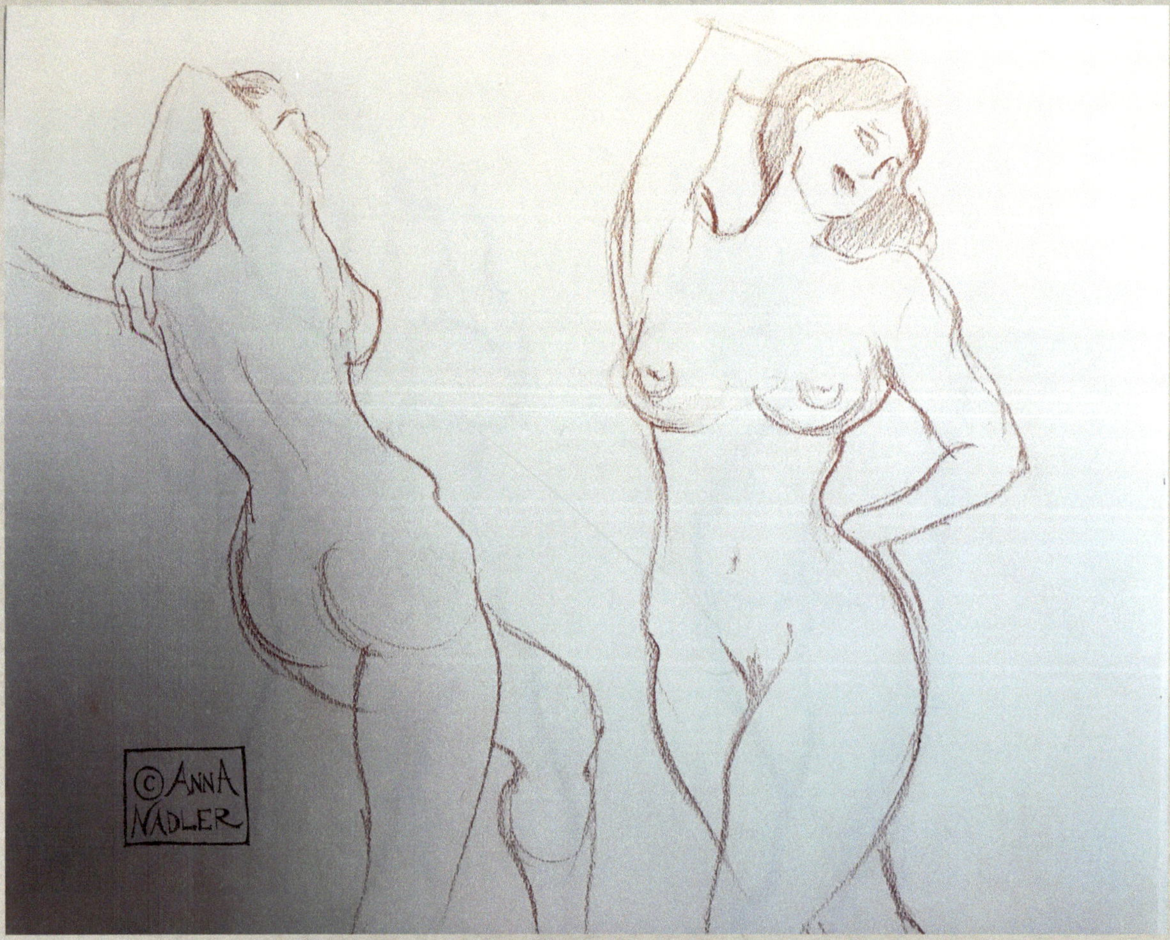

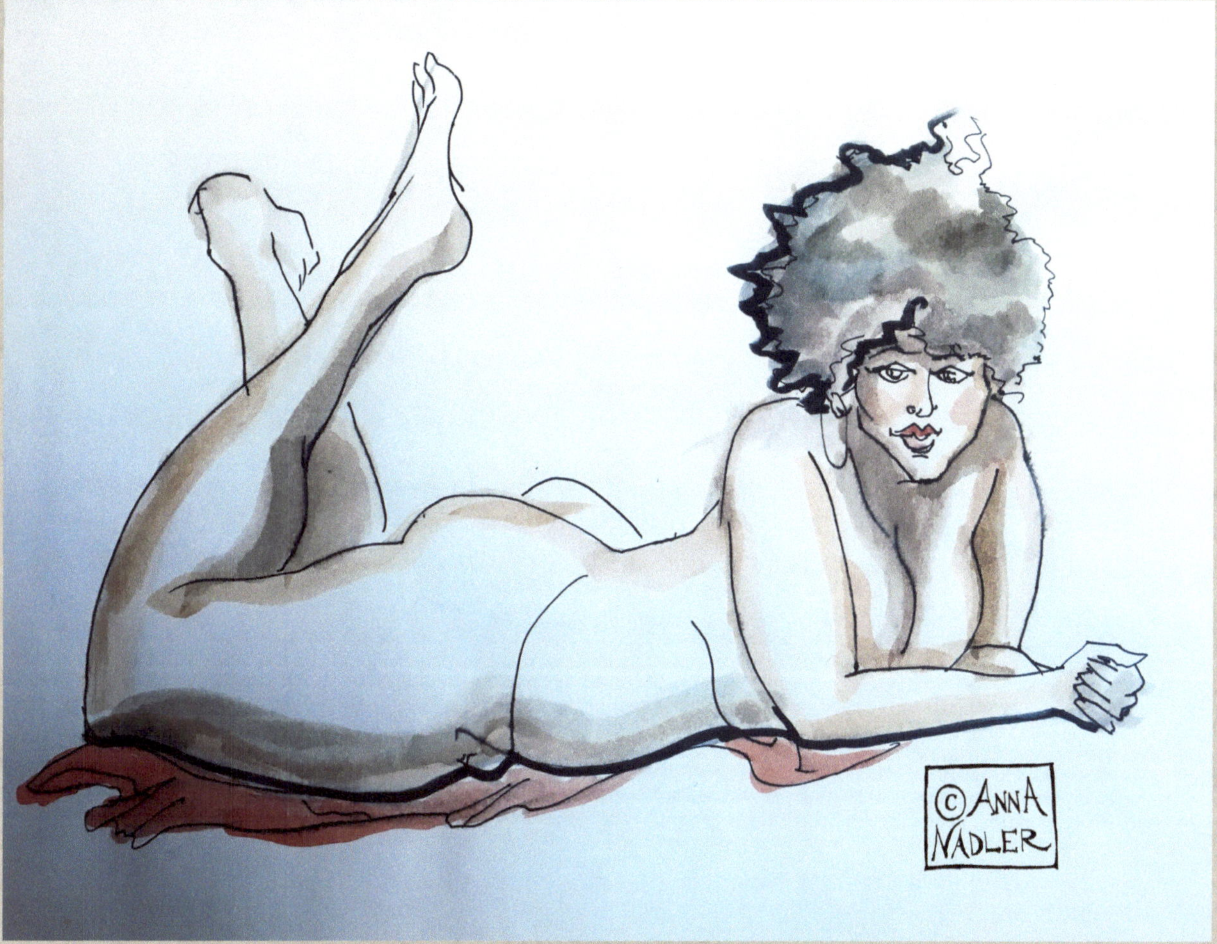

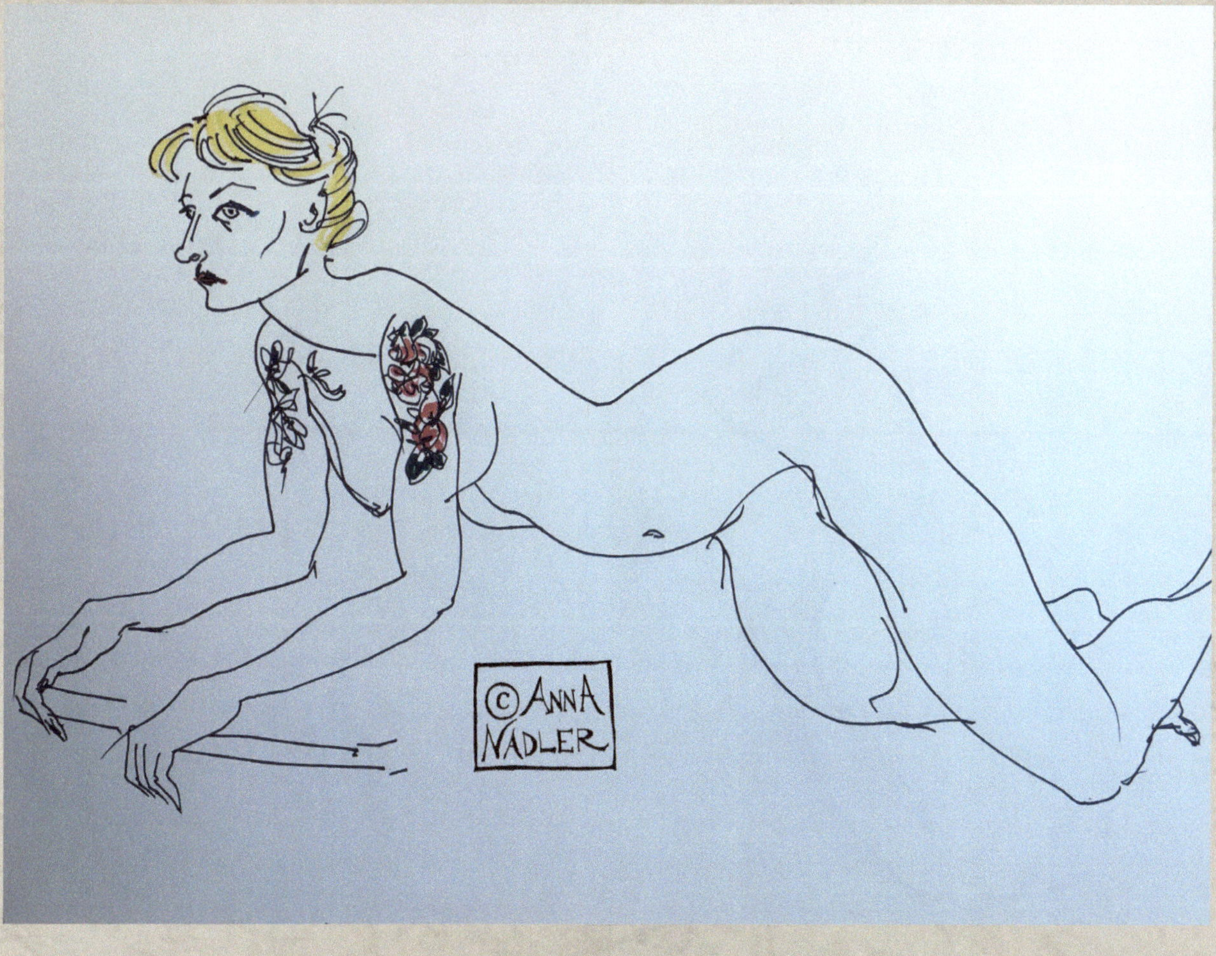

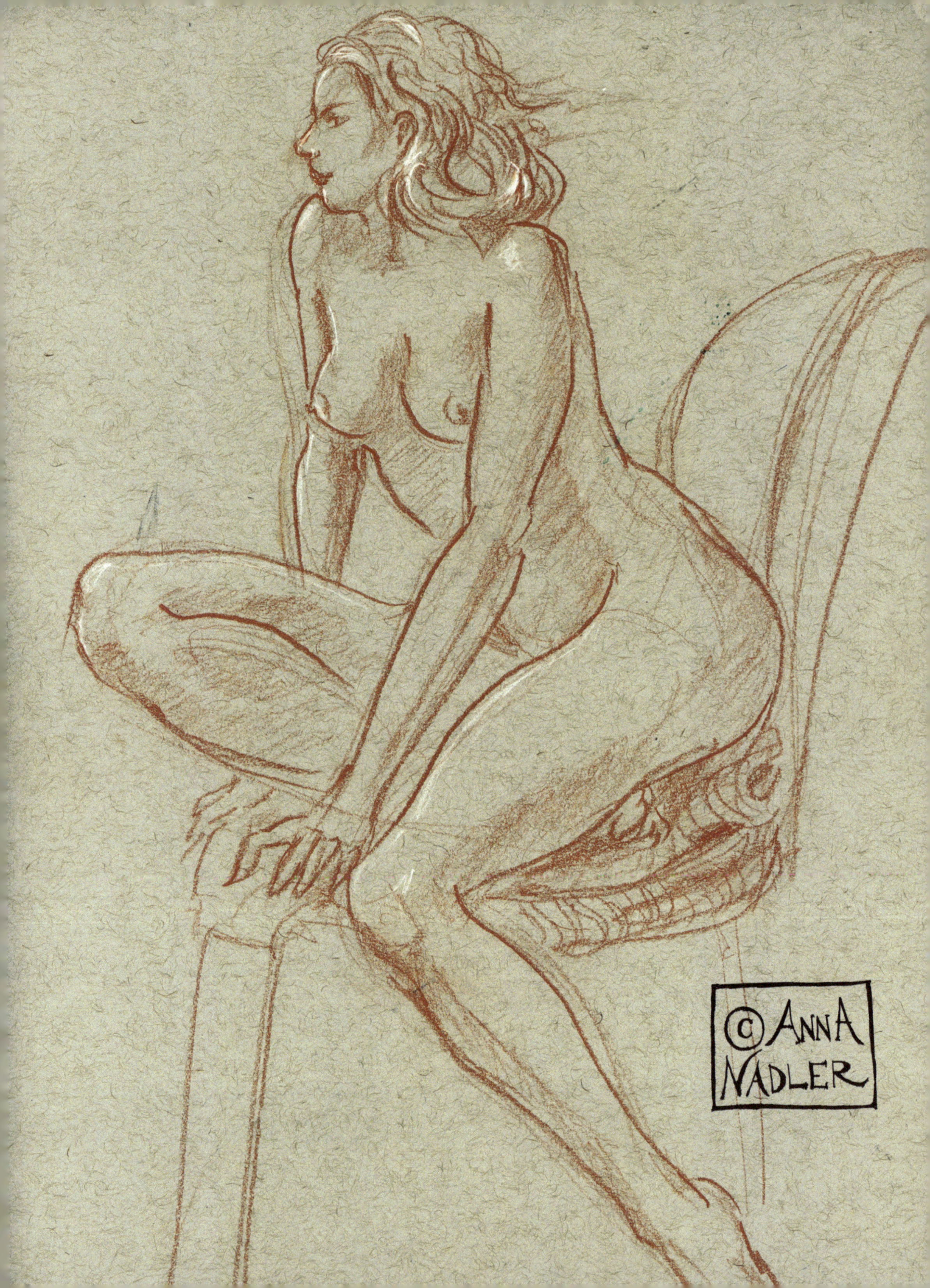

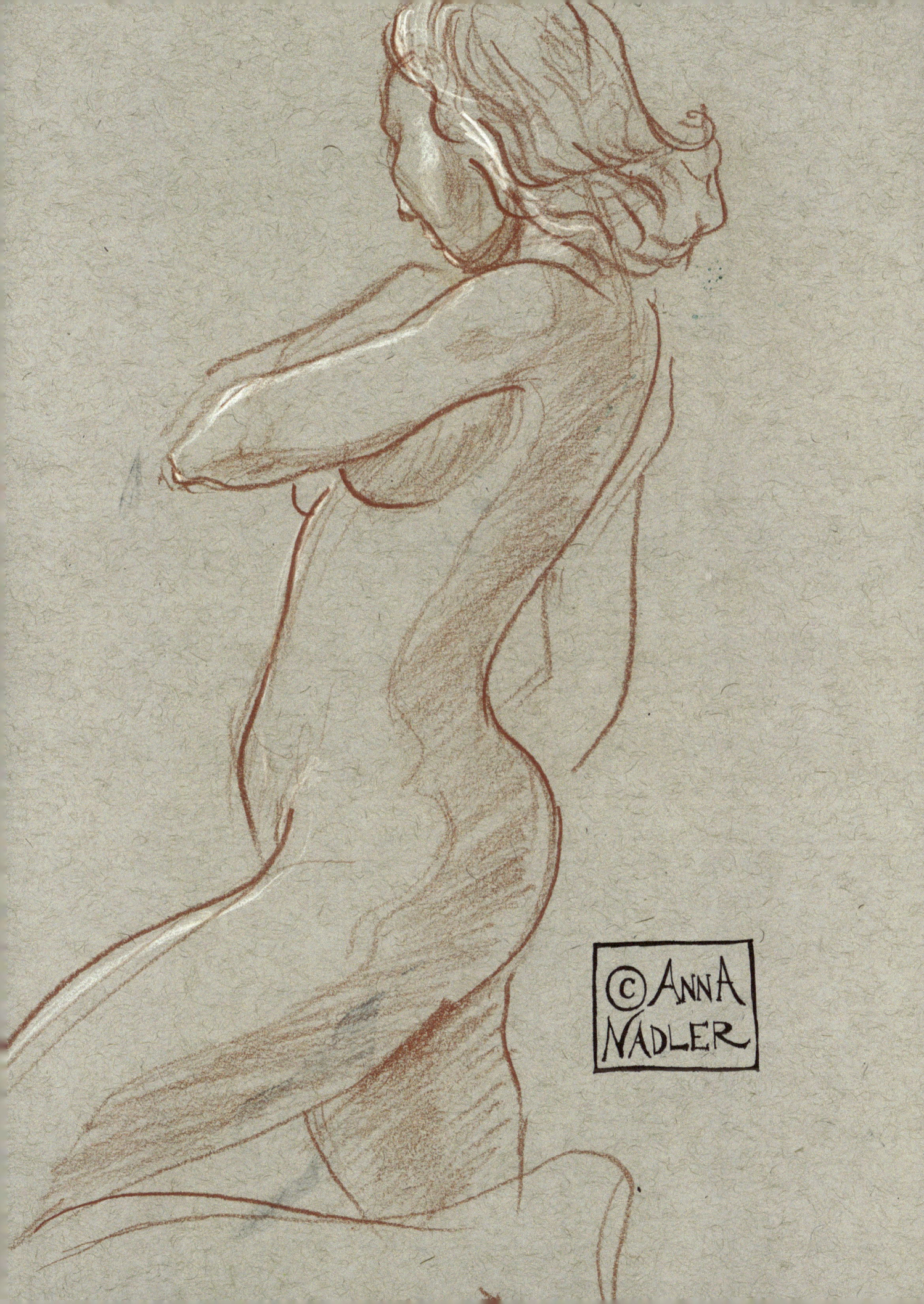

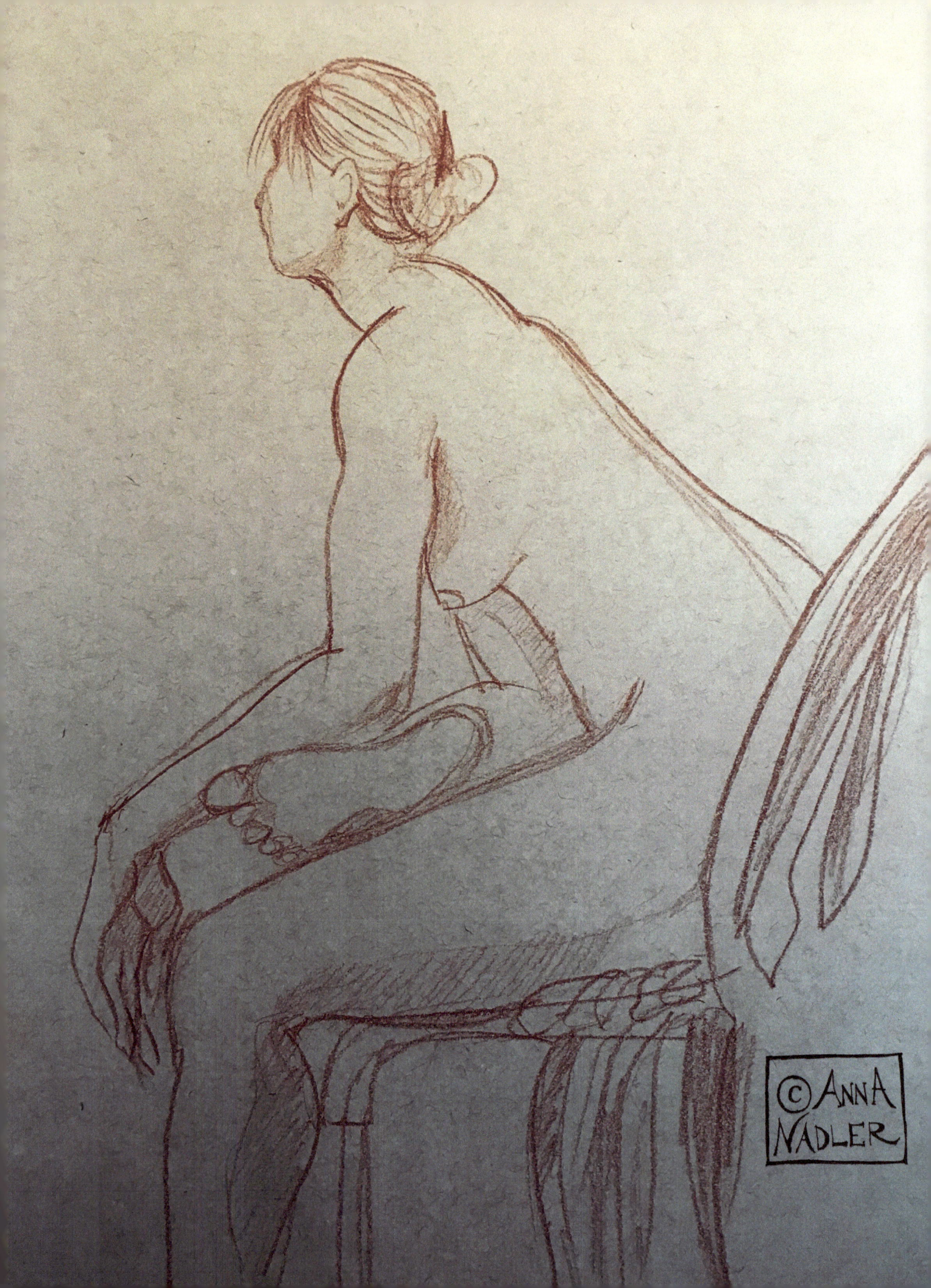

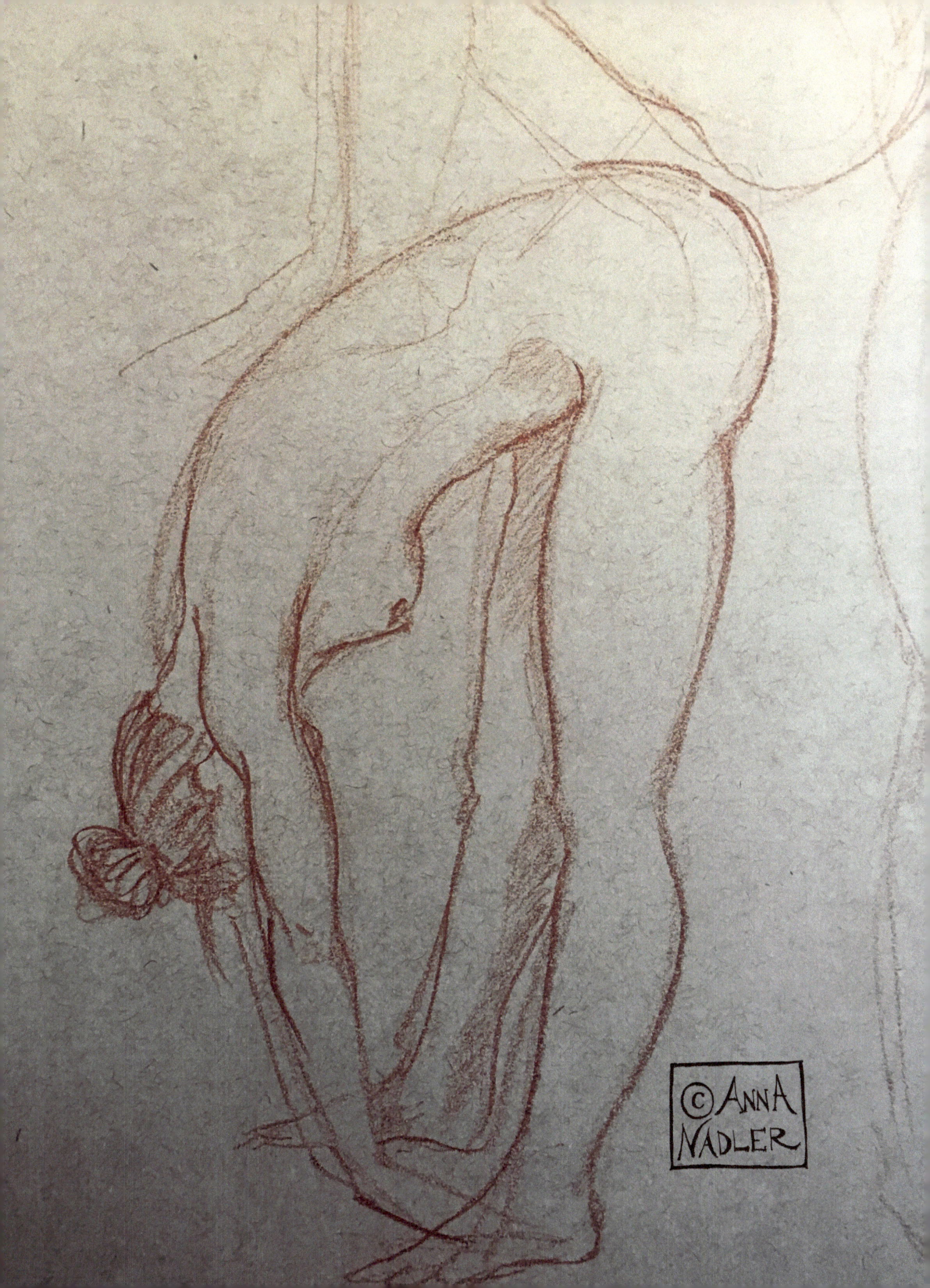

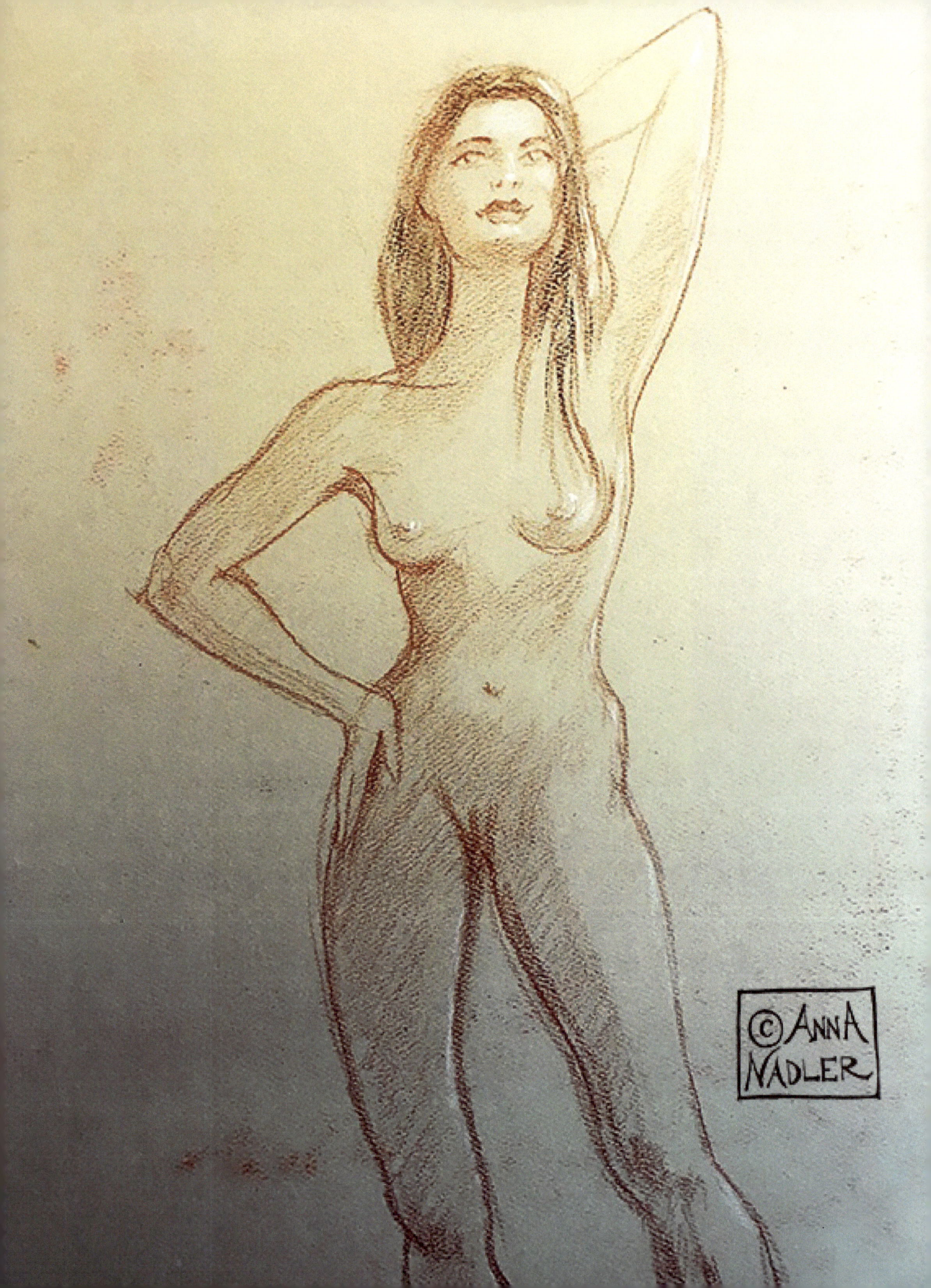

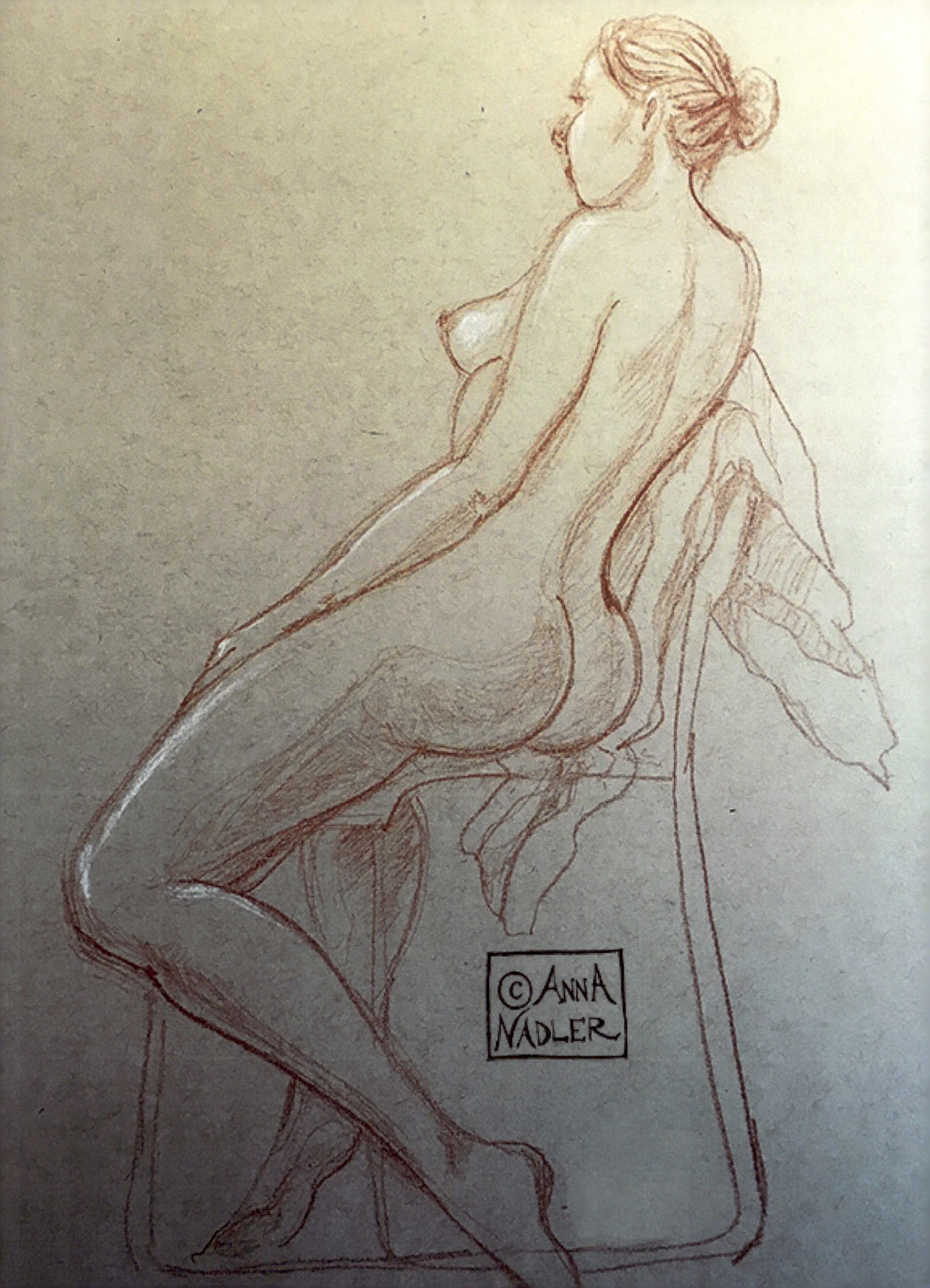

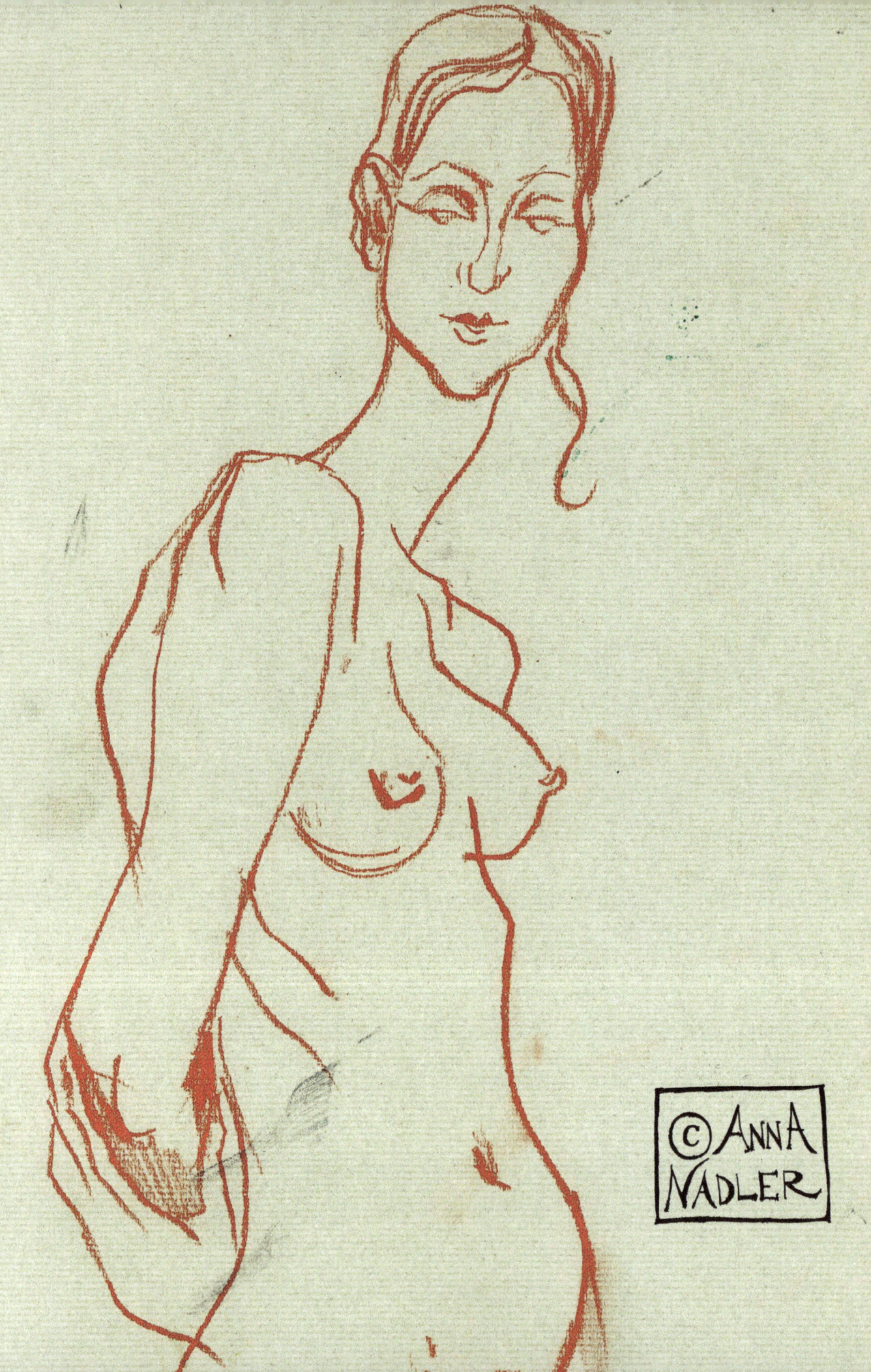

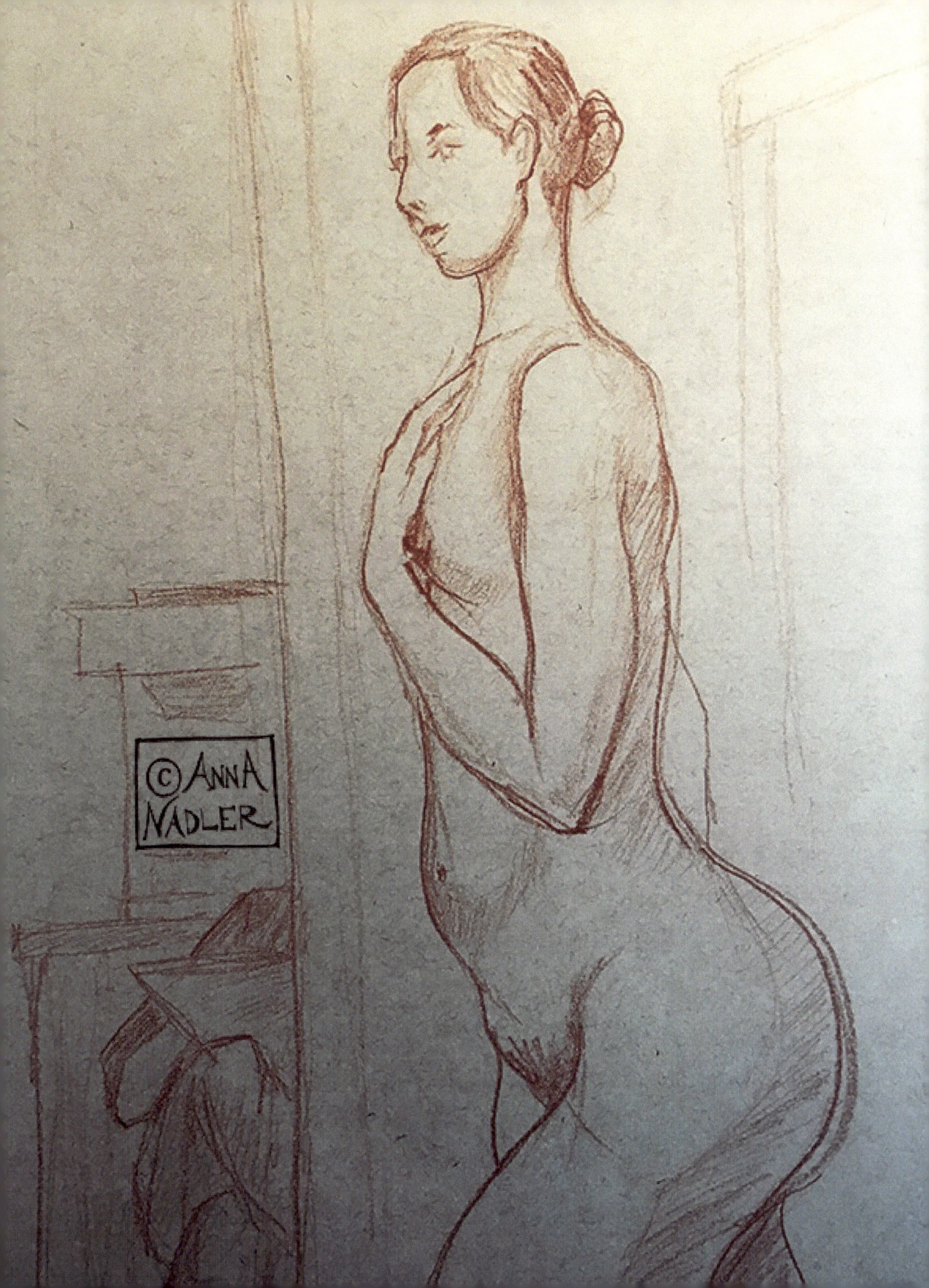

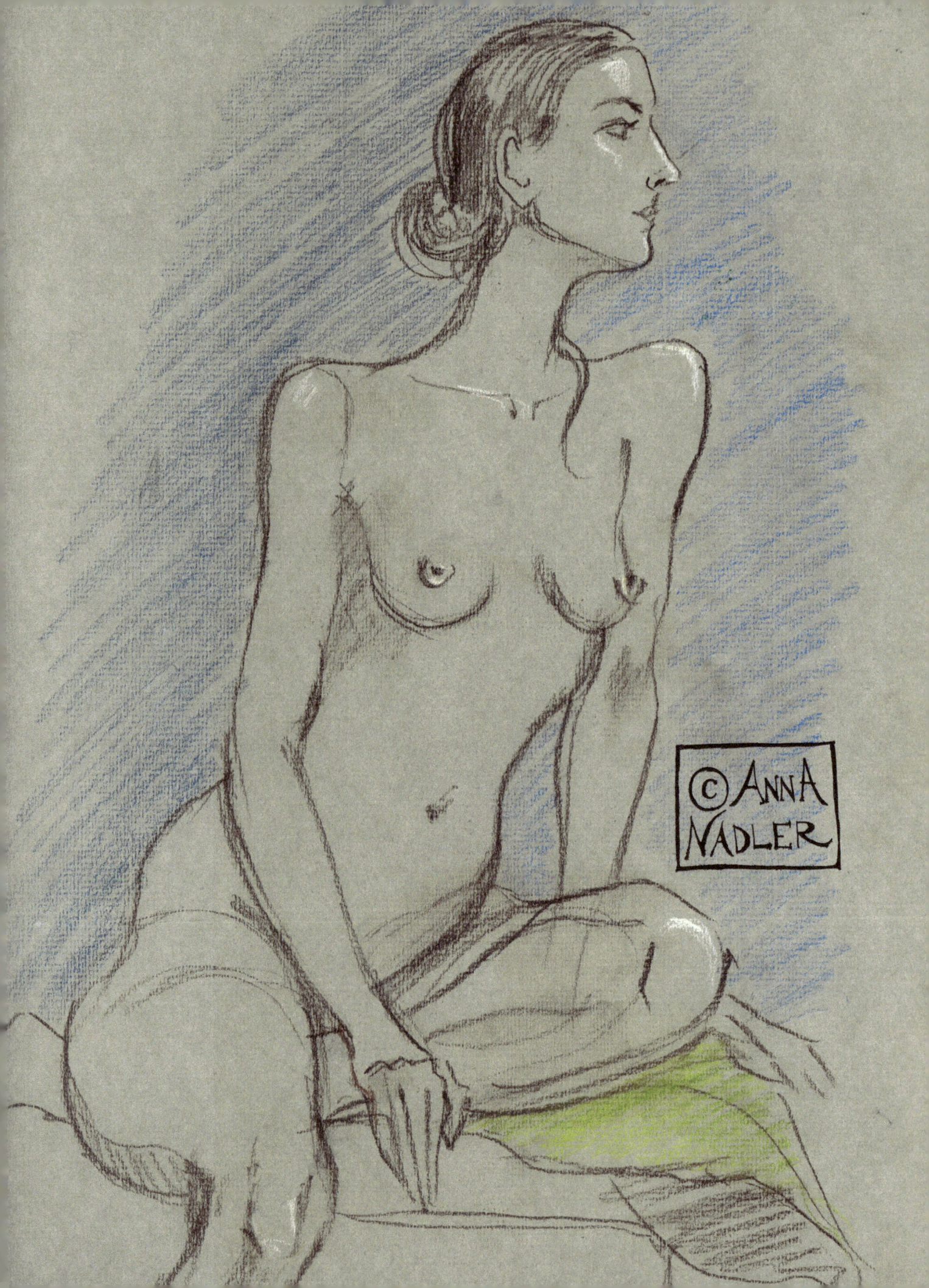

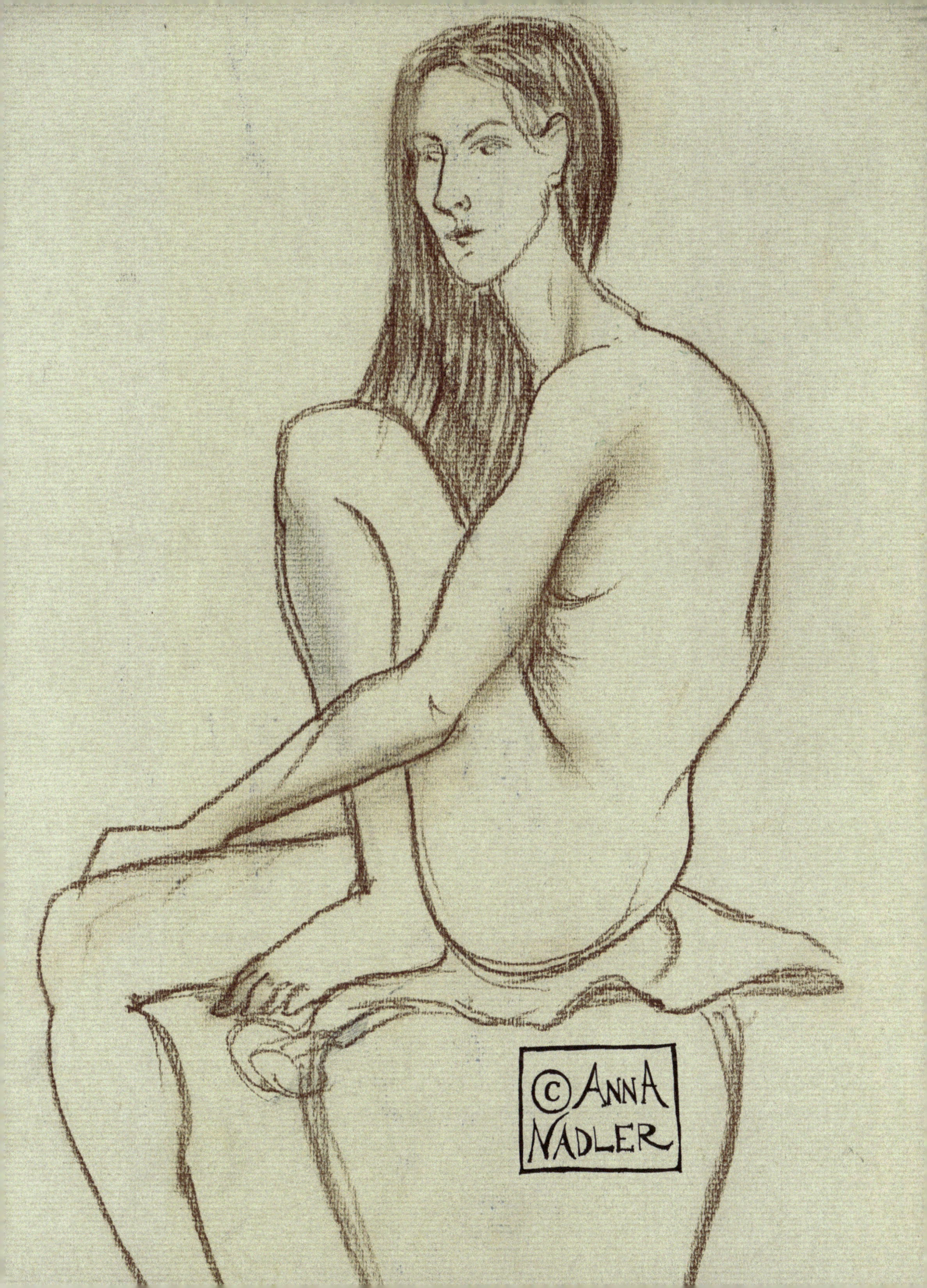

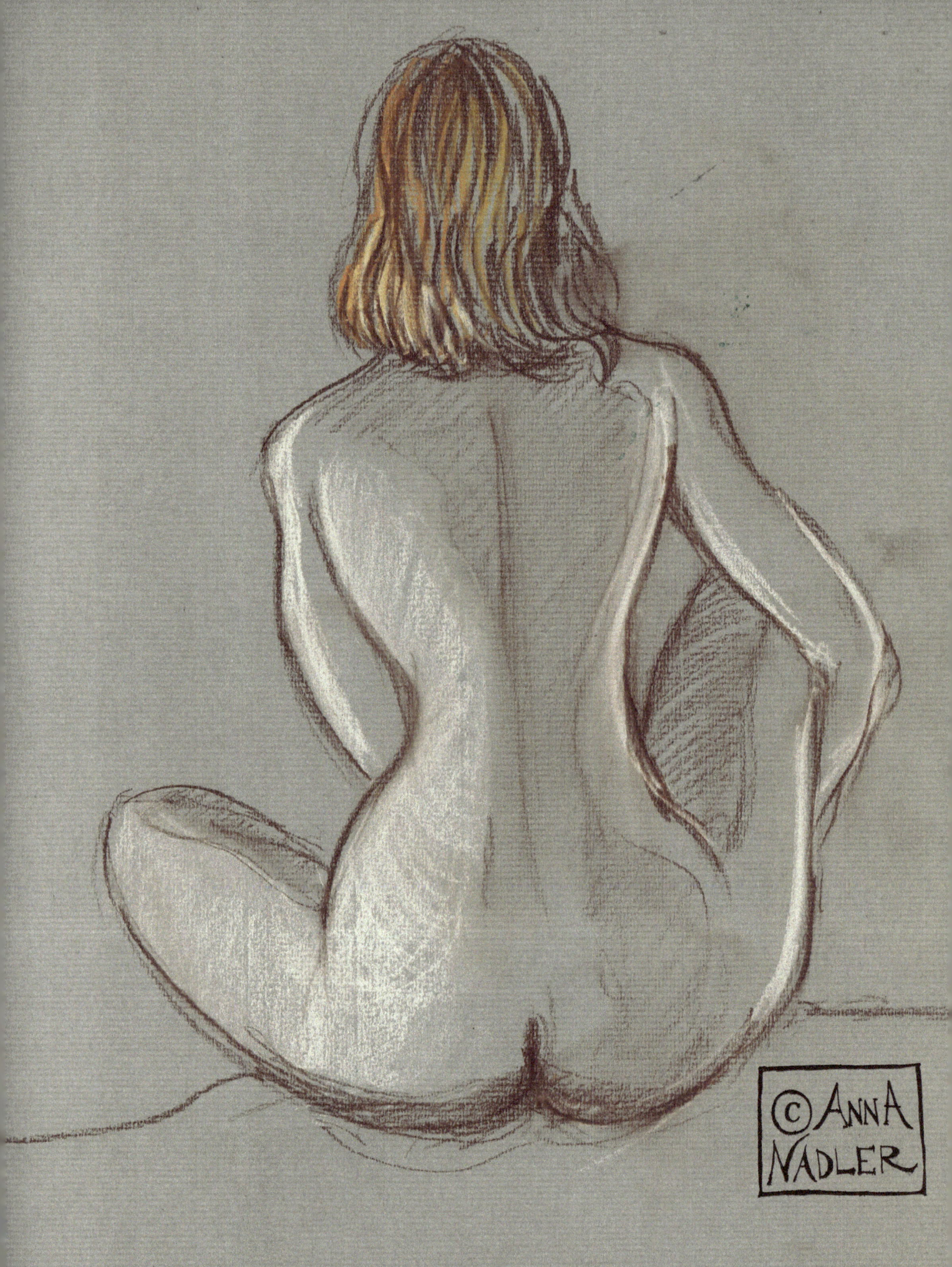

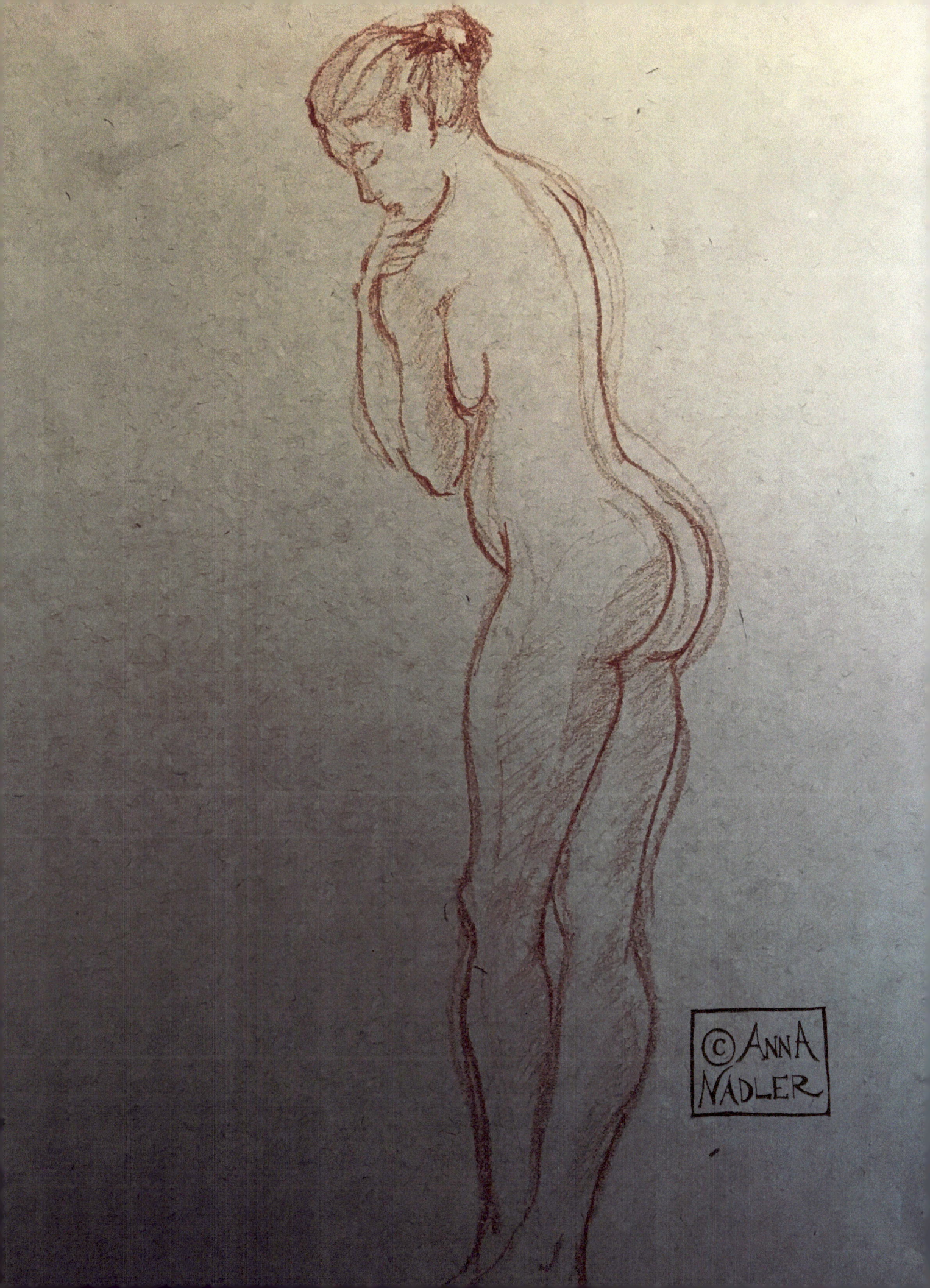

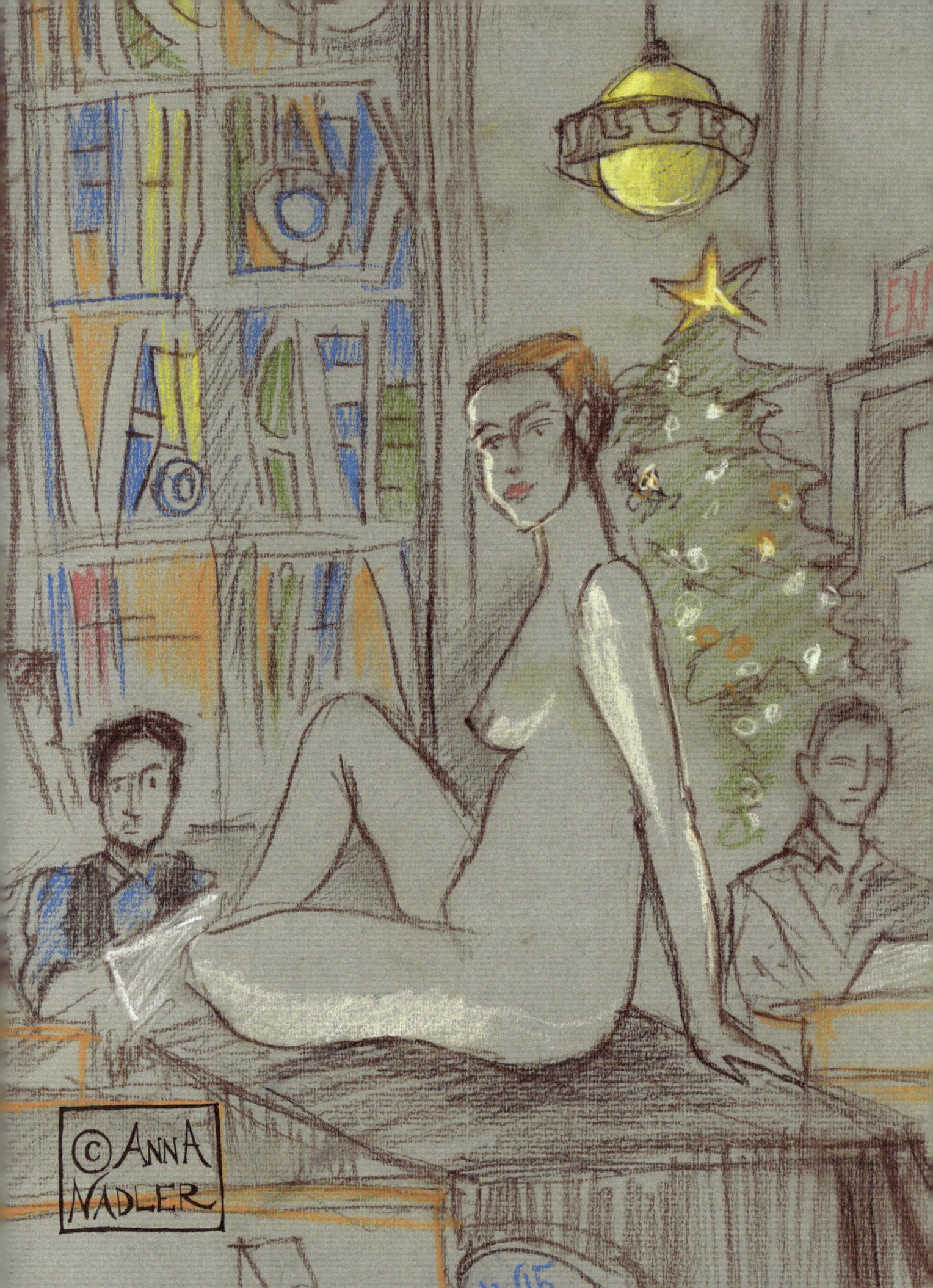

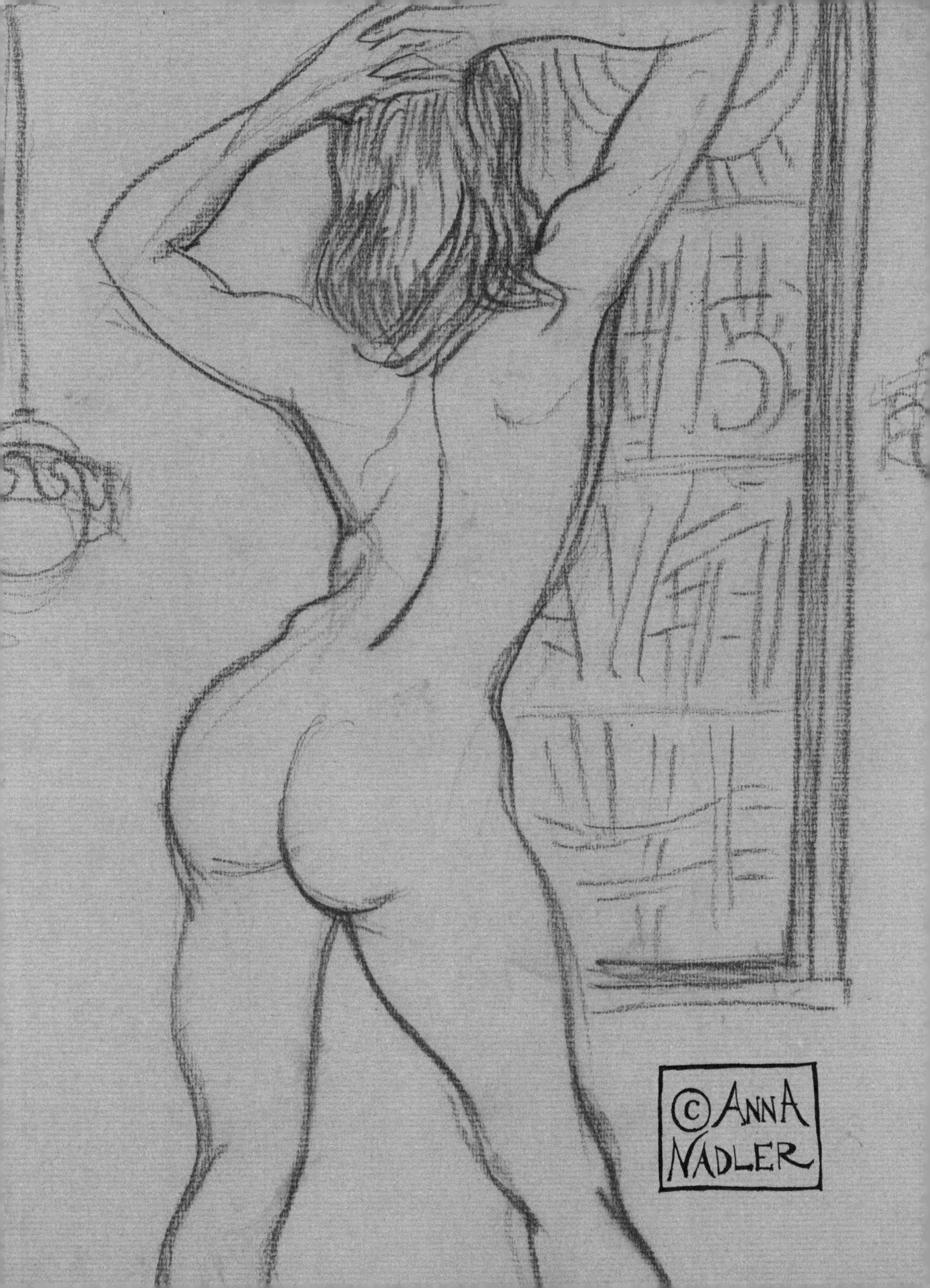

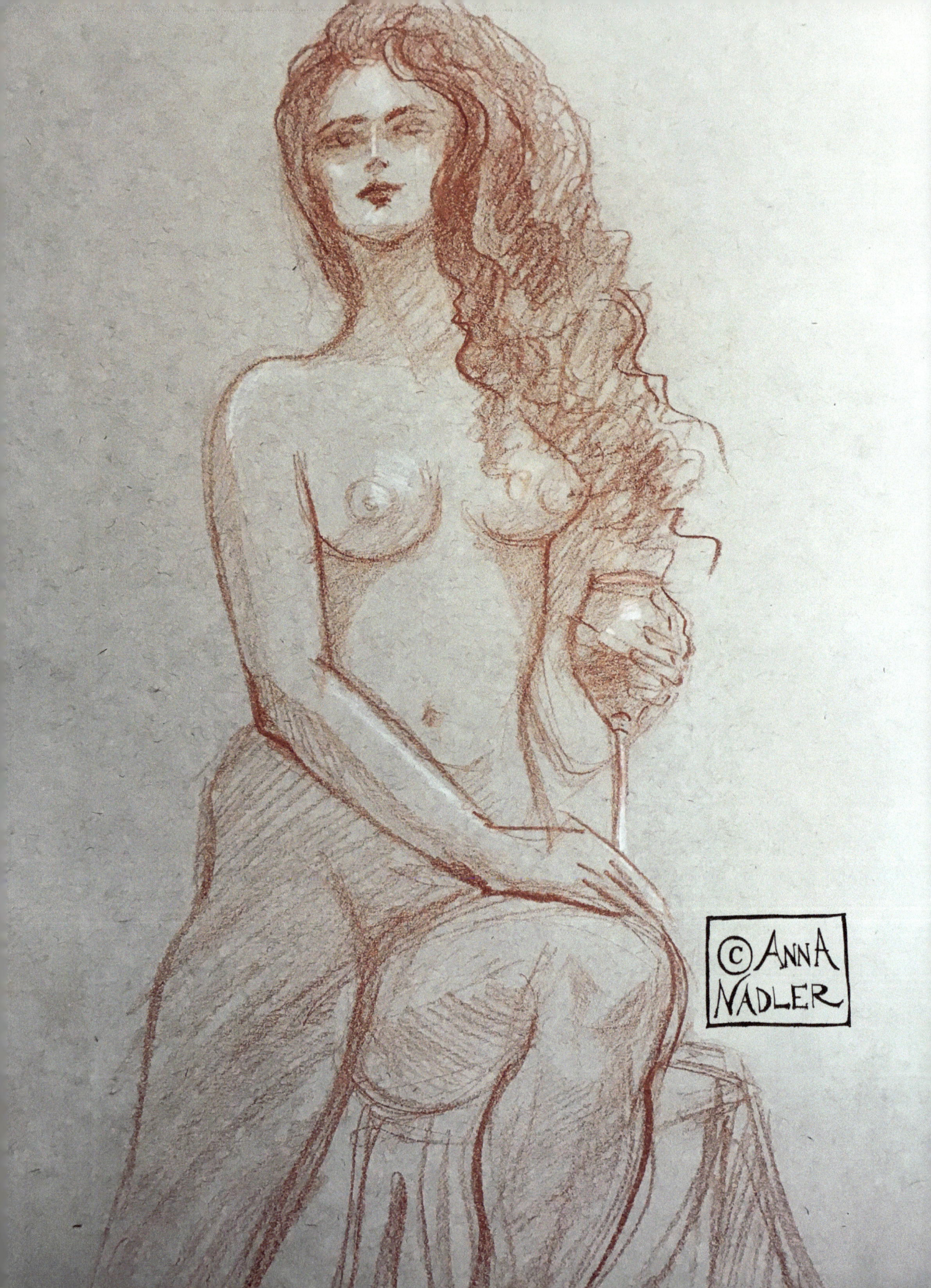

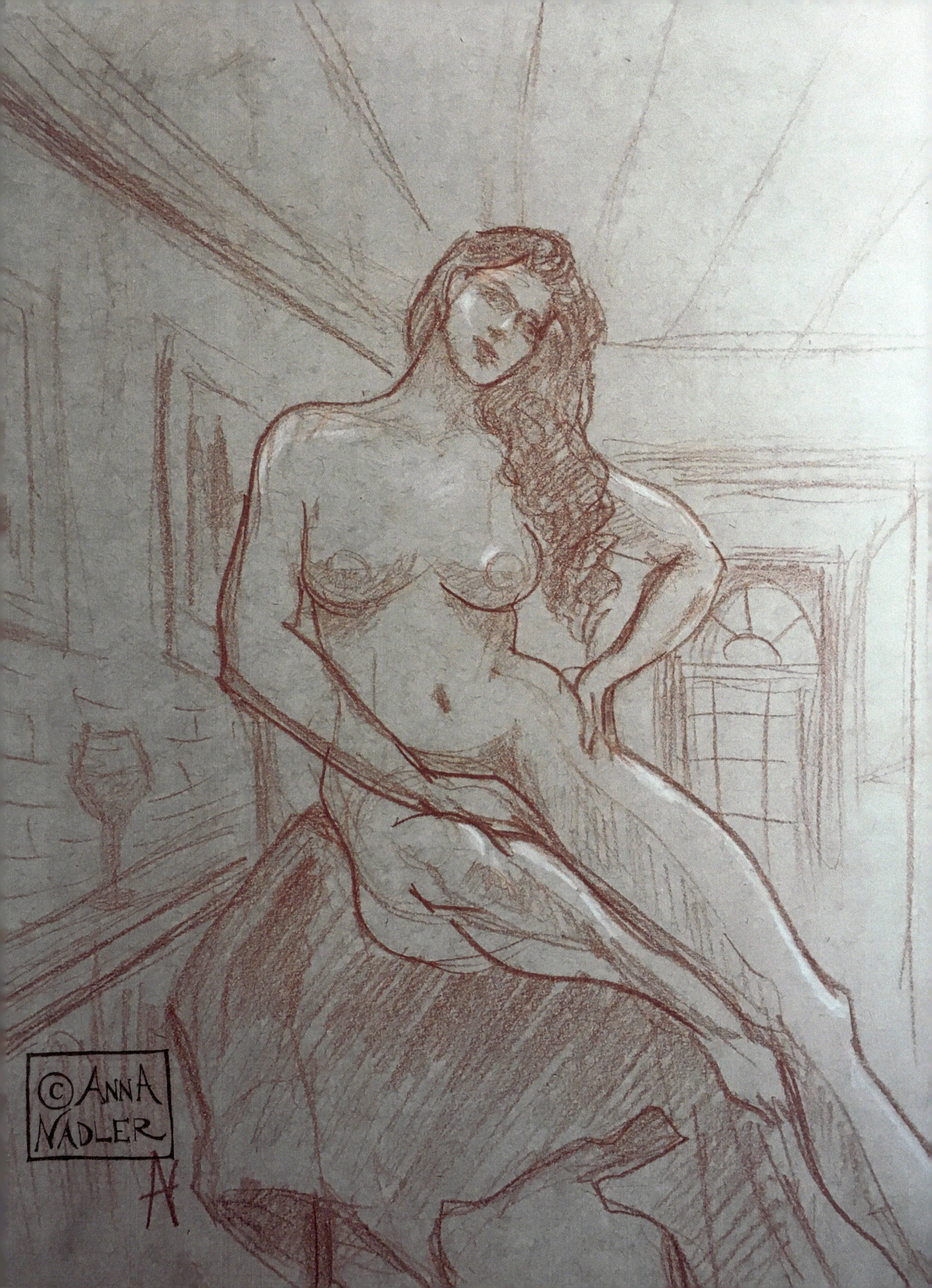

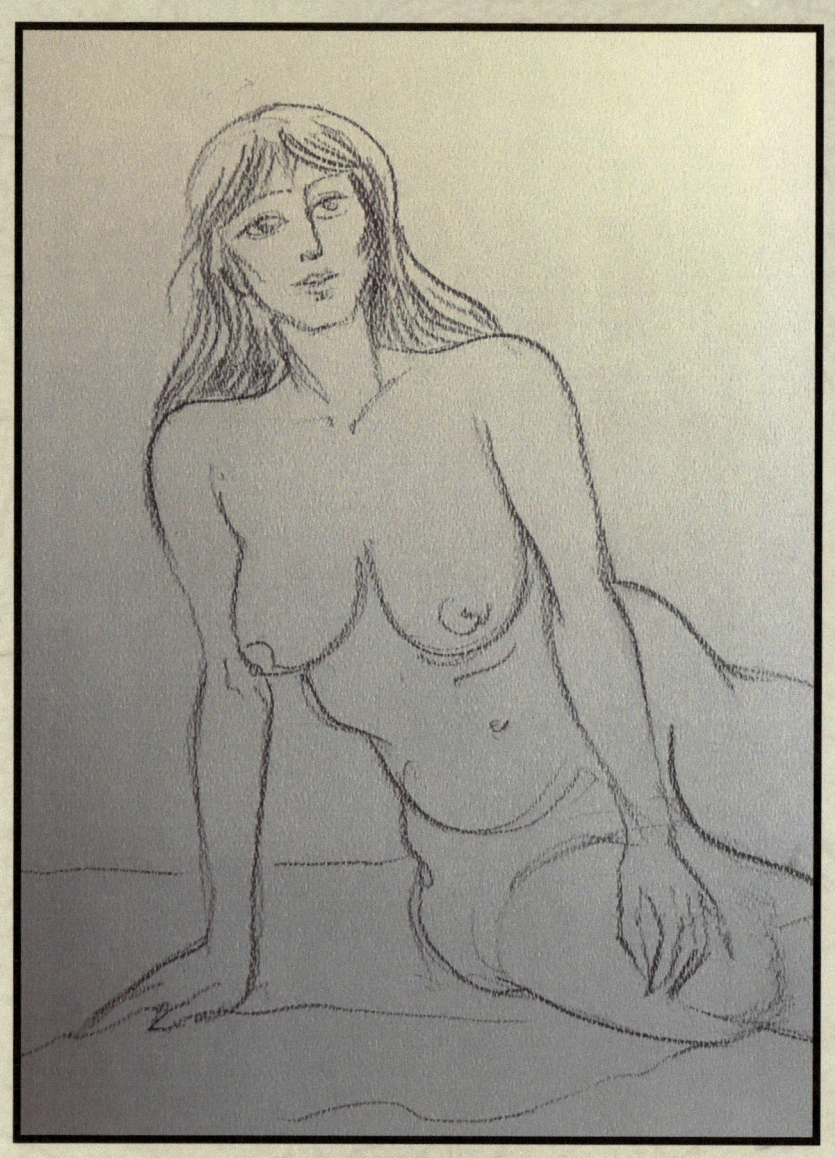

Thank you for viewing the collection
of "Drawing the Female Form."
If you enjoyed this book, please feel
free to leave a review on Amazon.com.

Thank you!

Anna Nadler